The Book of the Craft of Dying

Frances M. M. Comper

BIBLIOLIFE

THE BOOK OF THE CRAFT OF DYING

AND OTHER EARLY ENGLISH TRACTS CONCERNING DEATH

TAKEN FROM MANUSCRIPTS AND PRINTED BOOKS IN THE BRITISH MUSEUM AND BODLEIAN LIBRARIES

NOW FIRST DONE INTO MODERN SPELLING AND EDITED BY

FRANCES M. M. COMPER

WITH A PREFACE BY THE

REV. GEORGE CONGREVE, S.S.J.E.

LONGMANS, GREEN, AND CO.
39 PATERNOSTER ROW, LONDON
NEW YORK, BOMBAY AND CALCUTTA
1917

ALL THAT IS MINE IN THIS BOOK

I DEDICATE

TO THE LOVED MEMORY

OF ONE WHO HAS ALREADY

LEARNT THIS CRAFT

CONTENTS

PREFACE

THESE short treatises on the never-worn-out subject of Death are rescued from the shelves of the British Museum and Bodleian libraries.

The first, *The Craft of Dying*, is a translation of a very popular mediæval work *De arte Moriendi*, of which many versions exist, both in Latin and English. It offers to the Christian reader "A Commendation of Death," followed by chapters on the Temptations to which the last hours are subject, certain questions to ask in helping those that are near the end, certain suitable prayers for them, and an instruction for those that shall die.

There follows an early English translation of a chapter on Death from Henry Suso's *Horologium Sapientiæ*, which he himself translated from his earlier work *The little book of Eternal Wisdom.* It became a favourite book in the cloisters at the close of the Middle Ages, not only in Germany, but also in the Netherlands, France, Italy, and England.

The short chapter that follows is taken from a book entitled *The Toure of all Toures*, about which very little seems to be known.

The last treatise is *The Lamentation, or complaint of*

the Dying Creature, on the day when the Sergeant-of-arms, whose name is 'Cruelty,' comes from the Judge to arrest and to warn her to be ready at any moment to die, and to call to remembrance her sins and the goodness of God. In her fear and distress she appeals to her good Angel Guardian to answer for her, who replies that having counselled her too long in vain, she cannot help her now. Next she summons Reason, Dread, and Conscience to answer for her, but they dare not. Upon that she makes her complaint to her servants, the five senses, to say on her behalf the best they can ; but they decline, reproaching her with having always failed to discipline and control them. Upon this she sorrowfully betakes herself to *Faith* and *Hope* to be her advocates, and makes a belated appeal also to *Charity*, whom she had forgotten, that they would together bring her sad case before the Queen of Heaven for her intercession. Encouraged by these three friends she makes supplication to the Mother of Mercy, Mary, helper of succourless sinners. The little drama ends with the prayer of the Blessed Virgin to her Son for pardon for the sinful soul, and reconciliation with the Church before Death comes.

This presentation of death as mediæval Christianity saw it, and as it appears in the treatises here preserved, is naïvely sincere, full of awful anticipations of judgment, and of hope in the Divine mercy. It is interesting to compare it with the pagan representation of death found in classical literature. Lucian's adventures among the Shades are as entertaining as

Gulliver's travels: he never pretends for a moment to be in earnest. For example: Nireus,

> Comeliest of all that came 'neath Trojan walls,

contends there with Thersites for the palm of beauty, before Menippus the philosopher, who decides that between two skulls there is no distinction as to beauty, and sums up with, "Hades is a democracy; one man is as good as another here."

But this ironical and insolent tone is naturally exceptional. When men thought of death in the classical ages, they thought generally with what resignation they could of a state of gloom and unreality, in which life and hope were left behind. Their prevailing impression is expressed by Newman in his song "Heathen Greece":

> What the low beach and silent gloom,
> And chilling mists of that dull river,
> Along whose banks the thin ghosts shiver,—
> The thin wan ghosts that once were men,—[1]

And yet if death for pagan imagination implied nothing certain but emptiness and gloom, it is nevertheless generally referred to in the literature and inscriptions of those times with reverent awe, and tender memory, with the human pathos of bitter separation, and sometimes also with a manly spirit that faces the inevitable.

[1] *Verses on Various Occasions*, p. 305 (Longmans, Green & Co., 1890).

Here is Catullus' farewell at his brother's tomb:

> Nunc tamen interea prisco quæ more parentûm
> Tradita sunt tristes munera ad inferias,
> Accipe, fraterno multum manantia fletu:
> Atque in perpetuum, frater, ave, atque vale.

Or here is the Emperor Hadrian's address to his own soul about to depart this life:

> Animula vagula, blandula,
> Hospes comesque corporis,
> Quæ nunc abibis in loca,
> Pallidula, rigida, nudula?

Theocritus gives us this brave inscription on a seaman's tomb by the seashore:

> A shipwrecked sailor buried on this coast
> Bids you set sail;
> For many a gallant ship, when we were lost
> Weathered the gale.

There is the same vagueness as in the classical ages in what is written of death by Non-Christian authors of to-day; but they seem to have unconsciously absorbed some sweetness, and stray notes from the melody of Christian hope. The pathos and grace of the Hindu poet Tagore in his contemplation of death are irresistible.

"On the day when death will knock at thy door what wilt thou offer him?

Oh, I will set before my guest the full vessel of my life—I will never let him go with empty hands.

All the sweet vintage of all my autumn days and summer nights, all the earnings and gleanings of my busy life will I place before him at the close of my days when death will knock at my door.

. . . .

I have got my leave. Bid me farewell, my brothers! I bow to you all and take my departure.

Here I give back the keys of my door—and I give up all claims to my house. I only ask for last kind words from you.

We were neighbours for long, but I received more than I could give.

Now the day has dawned and the lamp that lit my dark corner is out.

A summons has come and I am ready for my journey.[1]

At this time of my parting wish me good luck, my friends! The sky is flushed with the dawn and my path lies beautiful.

Ask not what I have with me to take there. I start on my journey with empty hands and expectant heart.

I shall put on the wedding garland. Mine is not the red-brown dress of the traveller, and though there are dangers in the way I have no fear in my mind.

The evening star will come out when my voyage is done and the plaintive notes of the twilight melodies be struck up from the King's gateway.

. . . .

I was not aware of the moment when I first crossed the threshold of this life.

[1] *Gitanjali*, by Rabindranath Tagore, Nos. 90, 93 (Macmillan & Co.).

What was the power that made me open out into this vast mystery like a bud in the forest at midnight?

When in the morning I looked upon the light I felt in a moment that I was no stranger in this world, that the inscrutable without name and form had taken me in its arms in the form of my own mother.

Even so, in death the same unknown will appear as ever known to me. And because I love this life, I know I shall love death as well.

The child cries out when from the right breast the mother takes it away, in the very next moment to find in the left one its consolation."[1]

W. Pater gives us an impression of the strangely new attitude towards death which Christianity brought to men as Marius the Epicurean caught a glimpse of it on visiting a Christian cemetery: "'Januarius, Agapetus, Felicitas; Martyrs! refresh, I pray you, the soul of Cecilius, of Cornelius!' said an inscription. . . . 'Peace! Pax tecum!'—the word, the thought, was put forth everywhere, with images of hope. . . . The shepherd with his sheep, the shepherd carrying the sick lamb upon his shoulders. Yet these imageries after all, it must be confessed, formed but a slight contribution to the dominant effect of tranquil hope there—a kind of heroic cheerfulness and grateful expansion of heart, as with the sense, again, of some real deliverance, which seemed to deepen the longer one lingered through these strange and awful passages."[2]

[1] *Gitanjali*, by Rabindranath Tagore, Nos. 94, 95.
[2] *Marius the Epicurean*, vol. ii. p. 103 (Macmillan, 1909).

The Christian revelation in regard to the significance of death, and the awful change to which it opens, is the same for Christians of every age ; but in the way death is felt and spoken of by Christians of different ages one is conscious of some change of tone. In the New Testament references to the subject there is a very clear view of the victory which Christ won for every Christian by dying ; as in the Gospel story of His raising several persons to life ; in our Lord's words "I am the Resurrection and the Life" ; and in Saint Paul's desire to depart and be with Christ.

A very tender, hopeful and thankful tone prevails in the hymn for the dead by Prudentius in the fourth century :

> There let the sad complaint be dumb ;
> O Mothers, stay the falling tears ;
> Weep not your children's too brief years.
> Death but prepares for life to come.
>
> So buried seeds repair our store,
> Reorient from the parchèd earth,
> And teeming with their promised birth
> Blossom and burgeon as of yore.
>
> Take, Mother Earth, to sleep in dust,
> Cherish in no unfruitful rest,
> Quicken to life in thy soft breast,
> These noble relics I entrust.
>
> . . . .
>
> Take, Earth, consigned to thee this loan
> To be redeemed from sheltering sod,
> Not unremembered by its God,
> Who stamped His image on His own.
>
> . . . .

Redeemer, we Thy word obey,
  Who dying mad'st black death Thy thrall,
  And didst Thy Cross's partner call
To follow Thee along the way.

. . . .

These bones we'll guard with honour due,
  With violets deck the hallowed mould,
  The graven name, the marble cold,
With leaves and perfumes let us strew.[1]

The graver and more severe tone of the mediæval funeral rite appears in Saint Bernard's hymn "Cum sit omnis homo fœnum." :

Homo dictus es ab humo,
Cito transis, quia fumo
  Similis efficeris. . . .
O sors gravis! O sors dura!
O lex dira, quam natura
  Promulgavit miseris!
Homo nascens cum mœrore
Vitam ducis cum dolore
  Et cum metu moreris.

But this characteristic is nowhere so nobly expressed as in the majestic sadness of Notker's antiphon in the ninth century, *Mediâ vitâ*, translated by the English Prayer-book as follows, in the service 'at the Burial of the Dead': "In the midst of life we are in death: of whom may we seek for succour, but of Thee, O Lord, Who for our sins art justly displeased?

Yet, O Lord God most holy, O Lord most mighty,

[1] *Jam mæsta quiesce querela*, etc., transl. by F. St John Thackeray (Bell & Sons, 1890).

O holy and most merciful Saviour, deliver us not into the bitter pains of eternal death.

Thou knowest, Lord, the secrets of our hearts; shut not Thy merciful ears to our prayer; but spare us, Lord most holy, O God most mighty, O holy and merciful Saviour, Thou most worthy Judge eternal, suffer us not, at our last hour, for any pains of death to fall from Thee."[1]

The mediæval instruction for the priest attending a dying person naturally aims at the awaking in him a disposition of conformity to the will of God, and maintaining in him a penitential spirit. He is to be prepared to receive the sacraments worthily, Absolution on his confession, his Viaticum, the last Communion, and holy Anointing. The commendation of the parting soul, "Proficiscere anima Christiana de hoc mundo," expresses the profound solemnity of the preparation for death as it was felt in the middle ages. In accordance with this note we read of Saint Hugh of Lincoln[2] that as his end drew near "he bade his chaplain make a cross of ashes on the floor of his room, lift him from his

[1] Mediâ vitâ in morte sumus, quem quærimus adjutorem nisi te, Domine, qui pro peccatis nostris juste irasceris? Sancte Deus: Sancte Fortis, Sancte et misericors Salvator, amaræ morti ne tradas nos.

V. Ne projicias nos in tempore senectutis cum defecerit virtus nostra. Ne derelinquas nos Domine, Sancte Deus.

V. Noli claudere aures tuas ad preces nostras. Sancte Fortis.

V. Qui cognoscis occulta cordis: parce peccatis nostris.

[2] 1135-1200.

bed at the moment of his departure, and place him upon it. It was a November afternoon. The Choristers of St Paul's were sent for to sing Compline for him for the last time. He gave a sign when they were half through. They lifted him, and laid him upon the ashes. The Choristers sang on, and as they began the Nunc Dimittis, he died."[1]

Yet through the more characteristic tone of penetential sorrow, and fear of the last things, there may be caught also, throughout the middle ages, the note of victory over death. Thus we read of "The Passing of Saint Francis": "As the time of his death[2] drew nigh, the Blessed Francis caused himself to be stripped of all his clothing, and to be laid upon the ground, that he might die in the arms of the Lady Poverty. This done they laid him again on his bed, and as he desired they sang to him once more the Canticle of the Sun:

"'O most high, almighty, and good Lord God, to Thee belong praise, glory, honour, and all blessing.

Praised be my Lord for all His creatures; and especially for our brother the sun, who brings us the day, and brings us the light; fair is he and shining with a very great splendour; O Lord he signifies to us Thee.

Praised be my Lord for our sister the moon, and

[1] Froude's *Short Studies*, vol. ii. p. 99 (Longmans, 1884).

[2] A.D. 1226.

for the stars, the which He has set clear, and lovely in heaven.

Praised be my Lord for our brother the wind, and for air, and cloud, and all weather ; by the which Thou upholdest life in all creatures. Praised be my Lord for our sister water, and our brother fire.

Praised be my Lord for our mother the earth, the which doth sustain us, and keep us ; and bringeth forth diverse fruits, and flowers of many colours, and grass.

Praised be my Lord for all those who pardon one another for His love's sake, and who endure weakness and tribulation : blessed are they who peaceably shall endure, for Thou, O most Highest, shalt give them a crown.

Praised be my Lord for our sister the death of the body, from whom no man escapeth. Woe to him that dieth in mortal sin ! Blessed are they who are found walking by Thy most holy will ; for the second death shall have no power to do them harm.

Praise ye, and bless the Lord ; and give thanks to Him with great humility.'

On the morrow when his pains were some little abated, he bade call all the brethren that were in the place, and beholding them as they sat before him, he set his right hand upon the head of each, and gave his blessing unto all the Order present, absent, and to come, even unto the world's end.

Then as the sun was setting, there was a great silence. As the brethren were gazing on his face, desiring to see some sign that he was still with them, behold a great multitude of birds came about the house wherein he lay, and flying a little way off did make a circle round the roof, and by their sweet singing did seem to be praising the Lord with him."

A writer of to-day illustrates this trait of joy in death by the history of Saint Catherine of Siena[1] attending a condemned prisoner at his execution.

Nicolas Tuldo, condemned to death by the magistrates of Siena for political offences, was on his way to die on the scaffold outside his native town Perugia. One can imagine his despair, the natural revolt of his youth against his fate, his bitter regret for all he was going to lose. Catherine's visit to him was all that was needed to change those regrets into hope, that hope into joy. "Stay by me," he said, "and all will be well, and I shall be willing to die." Catherine promised to attend him to the place of execution, and Nicolas replied, "Whence comes so great a grace to me? What, will the comfort of my soul attend me to the dread place of justice? Yes, then I will go there gladly and in good heart; it seems to me as if I had yet a thousand years to wait before my death, when I think that you will be with me there." "At last he arrived," continues the saint, "as gentle as a lamb, and seeing me began to smile. He would have make me the sign of the cross on his forehead, and when he had received it, I said to him in a low voice, 'My dear brother go thou forth to the marriage feast to rejoice in the life that never ends.' He leaned forward with great gentleness, and I

[1] 1347-1380.

uncovered his neck ready for the blow of the axe. I had bent down to whisper him, and remind him of the blood of the Lamb of God that taketh away the sin of the world. His lips only replied 'Jesus, Catherine,' and as he said the words I received his head into my hands." Upon this the saint sees in vision our Lord receiving the blood, the soul of the penitent, and the fire of holy longing that grace had hidden in his heart,—sees Him welcome His penitent in the treasury of Mercy, His wounded Side; thus showing that it was by grace alone and not for any merit of his own that the Lord received the forgiven sinner. "O ineffable happiness," she adds, "to see how sweetly and lovingly the goodness of God welcomed the soul separated from the body. . . . The unction of the Holy Spirit that possessed this penitent overflowed him with joy enough to gladden a thousand hearts. It is no surprise to me for Tuldo tasted already the gentleness of God." [1]

Another example of joy in view of death in the middle ages is given in the account of the last days of Saint John of the Cross.[2] We read there that "on December 7th the surgeon in attendance told him on that day he had but few days to live. The saint answered with a joyful face in the words of the Psalmist. '*Lætatus sum*, etc.' 'I was glad when they said unto me we will go into the house of the Lord.' Then after a momentary pause, he added,

[1] *Vers la Joye*, by Lucie Felix-Faure Goyau, p. 276 (Perrin et Cie).

[2] 1542-1591.

'Since I have heard these good tidings, I feel no pain whatever.'"[1]

We recognise instinctively that the saint's joy could not be in the contemplation of the fact of dying, of dissolution. A later voice denies that in death itself there can be anything to desire :

> No man ever truly longed for death
> 'Tis life, not death, for which we pant,
> 'Tis life whereof our nerves are scant,
> More life and fuller than we want.

The saint's joy was in the attainment through death of that which made Saint Paul "desire to depart, and be with Christ." As Saint John of the Cross says elsewhere, "A principal reason why the soul desires to be released and to be with Christ, is that it may see Him face to face, and penetrate to the depth of His ways, and the eternal mysteries of His Incarnation."[2]

The more modern attitude towards death may be illustrated by John Bunyan (1684). He gives us in the *Pilgrim's Progress* his own individual and independent view, unhampered by Catholic tradition. He tells how the Pilgrims address themselves one after another to enter the river that separates them from the heavenly city,—the river that has no bridge.

Mr Despondency is one of the humblest of the

[1] v. *Life of St John of the Cross*, by David Lewis, ch. xxi. 280.

[2] *A Spiritual Canticle*, trans. by David Lewis, 2nd edit., 380 (Baker, 1891).

company. "When days had many of them passed away *Mr Despondency* was sent for. For a post was come and brought this message to him: *Trembling man, these are to summon thee to be ready with thy King by the next Lord's day, to shout for joy for thy Deliverance from all thy Doubtings.*

And said the Messenger: That my Message is true take this for a Proof; so he gave him the *Grasshopper to be a Burden unto him.* Now *Mr Despondency's* Daughter, whose name was *Much-afraid*, said, when she heard what was done, that she would go with her Father. Then *Mr Despondency* said to his Friends; 'Myself and my Daughter, you know what we have been and how troublesomely we have behaved ourselves in every Company. My will and my Daughter's is that our Desponds and slavish Fears be by no man ever received from the Day of our Departure for ever.' . . . When the time was come for them to depart, they went to the Brink of the River. The last words of *Mr Despondency* were: *Farewell Night, welcome Day.* His Daughter went through the River singing, but none could understand what she said."

Our thoughts of the last stage of the journey of life are enriched by the description of the wayfarers in the *Pilgrim's Progress* as one by one they prepare to pass out of this world. The book is a treasury of peculiarly English modern Christianity, its poetry, feeling, thought, and humour; but how much nearer to the height and depth of Gospel mysteries, to the solemnity of Holy Scripture dealing with the last things, and to its awful silence, does Newman attain throughout in his *Dream of Gerontius*. I do not refer to the details, or to the setting of the drama, but to the spirit of holy fear, of contrition, and of humble hope, that pervades it.

THE SOUL.

Take me away, and in the lowest deep
    There let me be,
And there in hope the lone night-watches keep,
    Told out for me.
There motionless and happy in my pain,
    Lone, not forlorn,—
There will I sing my sad perpetual strain,
    Until the morn.
There will I sing, and soothe my stricken heart,
    Which ne'er can cease
To throb, and pine, and languish, till possest
    Of its Sole Peace.
There will I sing my absent Lord and Love:—
    Take me away,
That sooner I may rise, and go above,
And see Him in the truth of everlasting day.[1]

I doubt whether there is anything in these mediæval counsels for the dying more characteristically reverent and tender than the few lines that follow from chapter ii. of *The Craft of Dying*.

"Therefore against despair, for to induce him that is sick and laboureth in his dying, to very trust and confidence that he should principally have to God at that time, the disposition of Christ on the Cross should greatly draw him; of the

[1] *Verses on Various Occasions*, pp. 366-7.

which Saint Bernard saith thus: 'What man is he that should not be ravished and drawn to hope, and have full confidence in God, if he take heed diligently of the disposition of Christ's body on the Cross. Take heed and see: His head is inclined to salve thee; His mouth to kiss thee; His arms stretched out to embrace thee; His hands pierced to give thee; His side opened to love thee; His body along strait to give all Himself to thee. Therefore no man should despair of forgiveness, but fully have hope and confidence in God; for the virtue of hope is greatly commendable, and of great merit before God. As the Apostle said and exhorted us: *Nolite amittere confidentiam vestram, quæ magnam habet remunerationem.* Lose not your hope and confidence in God, the which hath great reward of God.'"[1]

The following passage from Père Gratry gives us the Christian Faith in regard to death with the inimitable refinement of expression that distinguishes a saint of the most modern type in France.

The Master

I come without hesitation to the conclusion that above these multitudes that are for ever passing and disappearing, above that crowd of little stars, of souls intelligent and free, but as yet without form and veiled, God beholds, and is at work to gather out of that fluctuating mass an enduring

[1] *v.* p. 14.

heaven, firm and serene, where all that we have ever dreamed of good shall be found. And why? Because that eager reaching out towards God of the living reason, the soul's prayer, is but the effect of God Himself who beholds it,—of the attractive power of God, the working of God.

Disciple

Yes. . . . But one cannot deny either that those eager impulses of the soul and of reason are arrested and repressed by the spectacle of death.

The Master

The contrary would follow if one knew what death really is. Death is precisely that great force which sets us free to pass from earth to heaven, that is to say from a state of life that is uncertain, obscure, without form, to the new state for which we look. Death is the principal process of life. What is called life is the process that develops the starting point of the present. Death brings the new starting point.

Disciple

I understand. They are the two vital processes which the two processes in logic represent. The process of identity, which develops what one possesses already, corresponds with life: the process of transcendence, which lifts us up to higher principles, corresponds with death. By death there is a passing from life to a new and larger life. This is what in the bosom of earth appears by analogy in the succession of kinds that die, and are replaced by more perfect kinds.

Yes, death is the principal process in life,—its process of transcendence. It is the operation which, if it is not sadly mismanaged, will carry us on to God, and realise that wonderful word, "forsake thyself, and pass on to thy place in God and the infinite."

The Master

Very well. Death is then the supreme process ot life, since it delivers up the soul to God. It annihilates distance, the difference between its real and its ideal condition. In one sense it projects life from the finite to the infinite, not as if our created life could ever become infinite, but in the sense that death reunites it to its infinite source, and renders it established, full, and eternal.

So that the hideous dissolution of the body, and disappearance of the whole man which is called death, is in fact the annihilating of the obstacle that separated the real from the ideal life in God. . . .

Death, then, is no longer that incomprehensible enemy, that frightful phantom that the senses see in it. Death when well considered is for the real life of man what . . . for the life of the world is the true religion, and the working of the God Man, Who unites heaven and earth.[1]

[1] *La connaissance de l'âme.* Epilogue, p. 407. 5th Edition.

When, as in old age, the approaching end is long foreseen, could anything be more reverent and tender than Tennyson's welcome to death in "The silent Voices"?

When the dumb Hour, clothed in black,
Brings the Dreams about my bed,
Call me not so often back,
Silent Voices of the dead,
Toward the lowland ways behind me,
And the sunlight that is gone!
Call me rather, silent Voices,
Forward to the starry track
Glimmering up the heights beyond me
On and always on!

Or in his "Crossing the Bar":

Sunset and evening star,
  And one clear call for me!
And may there be no moaning of the bar,
  When I put out to sea,

But such a tide as moving seems asleep
  Too full for sound and foam,
When that which drew from out the boundless deep
  Turns again home.

Twilight and evening bell,
  And after that the dark!
And may there be no sadness of farewell,
  When I embark;

For tho' from out our bourne of Time and Place
  The flood may bear me far,
I hope to see my Pilot face to face
  When I have crost the bar.

But when death comes in the most tragical guise,

as when helpless crowds sink in a torpedoed ship, see how Christian character ennobles what is merely horrible:

"Father Maturin's end was that of a hero. And by a happy chance we know some of its details. After luncheon on that fated Friday, May 7th, at about two o'clock he was seen on the deck saying his office. The torpedo struck the ship soon after two. How long it took him to realise to the full what had happened, we do not know, but we do know from a lady who survived that shortly before the ship went down twenty minutes later, he was seen striving to keep people calm, giving absolution to those who asked for it, fastening on life-belts, and helping women and children into the boats. The lady who relates this was herself helped into a boat by Father Maturin, and just as the boat was putting off he threw a little child into her arms, with the injunction 'try to find its mother.' Then he stood waiting for the end quite calm, but as white as a sheet. With his keen sense of the drama of life he probably realised vividly the approaching end. He put on no life-belt. He did not take off his coat. He made no attempt to escape, but simply awaited death. We can picture him then, as ever, intensely human, and intensely spiritual—realising keenly that his own death was now a matter of minutes, yet eager to the last to do good and help others, and throwing himself on God for strength and support." [1]

[1] Introduction by Wilfrid Ward to sermons by Father Maturin (Longmans).

Among the prophets of our time Browning goes to meet death, as our men in France to-day spring from their trench at a signal, and cross the deadly space between them and the enemy's first line.

> I was ever a fighter, so—one fight more,
> The best and the last!
> I would hate that death bandaged my eyes and forebore,
> And bade me creep past.
> No! let me taste the whole of it, fare like my peers
> The heroes of old,
> Bear the brunt, in a minute pay glad life's arrears
> Of pain, darkness, and cold."

Or

> . . . There they[1] stood, ranged along the hill-sides,—met
> To view the last of me, a living frame
> For one more picture! in a sheet of flame
> I saw them and I knew them all. And yet
> Dauntless the slug-horn to my lips I set
> And blew, "*Childe Roland to the Dark Tower came.*"

Or if all natural powers are outlived in old age, and nothing remains but the remembrance of things past, death is contemplated only as the end of weariness and a door of hope.

> So, at the last shall come old age.
> Decrepit as befits that stage;
> How else wouldst thou retire apart
> With the hoarded memories of thy heart,
> And gather all to the very least
> Of the fragments of life's earlier feast,
> Let fall through eagerness to find
> The crowning dainties yet behind?

[1] *i.e.* the dead leaders of lost causes.

Ponder on the entire past
Laid together thus at last,
When the twilight helps to fuse
The first fresh with the faded hues,
And the outline of the whole,
As round eve's shades their framework roll,
Grandly fronts for once thy soul!
And then as, 'mid the dark a gleam
Of yet another morning breaks,
And like the hand that ends a dream,
Death with the might of his sunbeam
Touches the flesh and the soul awakes,
Then—[1]

Mrs Browning refuses to contemplate death : "I cannot look on the earthside of death. When I look deathwards I look over death, and upwards, or I can't look that way at all." And has she not some ground for this in the Lord's word : "I am the Resurrection and the Life. . . . Whosoever liveth and believeth in Me shall never die" ?

And some there are who seem to be carried through death as a babe fast asleep in his mother's arms.

Thus in "A Death in the Desert."

We had him, bedded on a camel-skin,
And waited for his dying all the while;
This did not happen in the outer cave
But in the midmost grotto: since noon's light
Reached there a little, and we would not lose
The last of what might happen on his face.
. . . We laid him in the light where we might see :
For certain smiles began about his mouth,
And his lids moved, presageful of the end.
But he was dead . . .

[1] *The Flight of the Duchess.*

> Ye will not see him any more
> About the world with his divine regard!
> . . . . . . and now the man
> Lies as he lay once, breast to breast with God.

But the present war with its unprecedentedly numerous casualties seems not seldom to invade and lay bare the inscrutable mystery of death as never before. How often of late we have had our revelations? How often we have seen the light that dawns as this world's light dies?

The Abbé Klein finds a young French officer, a boy of twenty, brought into hospital desperately wounded; half of the brain laid bare, and a paralysis setting in. He could not question him much, but elicited his parents' address, and "I communicated at Easter and after I was wounded." "Your sufferings are great, resign yourself to them."—"God's will be done." "Then," writes the Abbé, "I knew enough. I suggested to him an act of love to God, and gave him absolution without confessing him again, and then the Blessed Sacrament. He received the sacrament with a joyous light in his eyes, usually so dim, and afterwards at each visit while I held his hand, our eyes would meet in a long look. When I came the nurse would often tell me that he no longer seemed conscious of anything. All the same I would suggest to him, 'My friend let us pray': 'My God I love Thee.' And always he would stir from his apparent torpor long enough to repeat, 'My God I love Thee.' The first day he added of his own accord after a moment's pause this one little word, which shed a ray of pure light on the depths of his silence. 'My God I love Thee—dearly.'

The last morning unable to speak, he made the sign of the Cross.

What precious times we had together. I would not have exchanged them for all the lessons of the greatest teachers in the world.

Atonement, it was indeed there in all its sadness and all its beauty in the person of this gentle, wounded boy of twenty, who had endured this terrible wound without complaint, and from the first had offered up all his sufferings to God, and now was passing to his death so slowly through the long days and longer nights without breaking his silence except to say 'My God I love Thee.' It is through such sacrifices that the salvation of races is won, and our iniquities redeemed. . . .

Death our benefactor, our deliverer, working our perfection not our destruction! Thou who art the supreme victory, pardon the folly that calls thee a calamity. And praised and blessed for ever be Atonement, the greatest work of the Love of God, which blots out all the stain of evil, and, not content with adding lustre to the crown of the Blessed, opens a way into heaven for the very sinners themselves." [1]

Or read a French soldier's letters to his mother:

"I had often enough known the joy of seeing a spring come like this, but never before had I been given the power of living in every instant. So it is that one wins, without the help of any science, a

[1] *Hope in Suffering*, Abbé Klein, pp. 245-6.

vague, but indisputable intuition of the Absolute. . . . These are hours of such beauty that he who embraces them knows not what death means. I was well in advance of the front line, but I never felt better protected.

This morning the sun rose red and green over the snow that was ruddy and blue ; there was a wide expanse of fields and woods recovered into life, and far away the distance in which the silver of the Meuse died away. Oh Beauty ! Beauty *quand même*."

"I have just lost my dearest friend," he writes. "Dear, dear mother ; there is only one feeling left, —love." To the end he keeps this stern faith. "The regiment next to ours has but forty men left to it. I dare not speak any more of hope. What one can demand is that one should have grace to exhaust all that the instant holds of good."

He was lost in his last fight : and was never heard of more. His last message had been :—

"DEAREST MOTHER,—It is mid-day, and we are at the last moment before the assault. I send you all my love. Whatever happens life has had its beauty. . . . I leave you to God. I kiss you without any further word. All my being is bent on its hard task. Good-bye. Hope against hope, but above all, hold by wisdom and love."[1]

So day after day mothers and sons part in the

[1] *v.* H. S. H. in the *Commonwealth*, Jan. 1917.

dark, separated by death, never to meet again in this world. Their last words imply the great obscurity, the unspoken question, what will death be? to which no answer ever comes. But the Christian soldier does not stop to seek replies. "I leave you to God," he says in his good-bye. "*Hope against hope, hold fast by love,*" and goes forward in the way of duty right into the cloud. His hope has a sure intuition that the cloud hides the divine Love, that it is Love he will meet in death, that we cannot know death's secret beforehand, because it is too good to be known till the day dawn. But as he goes straight on to face whatever may be before him, love reveals more than hope can, for love is a mystical possessing *now* of all that hope looks for in the future, love is a personal fellowship of the soul with God in Christ enjoyed already.

The obscurity remains for us all while we sit still and wait for it to lift.

> There lives no record of reply
> That telling what it is to die
> Had surely added praise to praise.

We stoutly refuse belief to the adventures of mediums in the spiritual world. But the Christian listens intently to the high thoughts of our noblest teachers who have spoken to us of death, not with certainty or by revelation, but as Saint Paul when he gave us his best convictions *as his own*, and added, "*But I think I have the spirit of God.*" Who of us does not desire to know what the poet Wordsworth's thoughts

*

were about death? We listen keenly as his sonnet sings them:

Methought I saw the footsteps of a throne
Which mists and vapours from mine eyes did shroud—
Nor view of who might sit thereon allowed;
But all the steps and ground about were strown
With sights the ruefullest that flesh and bone
Ever put on: a miserable crowd,
Sick, hale, old, young, who cried before that cloud,
"Thou art our king, O Death! to thee we groan."
I seem'd to mount those steps; the vapours gave
Smooth way: and I beheld the face of one
Sleeping alone within a mossy cave,
With her face up to heaven; that seemed to have
Pleasing remembrance of a thought foregone;
A lovely Beauty in a summer grave!

We are touched and cheered indeed, but the noblest guesses leave the secret of death undisclosed. We leave it without anxiety, for we leave it with God, Who is not merely the Arbiter, but the Father and lover of souls; sure at least of this that the revelation when the cloud lifts, will be lovelier than our loveliest thoughts about it; for we are convinced that it is not merely some benevolent purpose of God that death has to reveal to the loyal soul that goes forward into the dark to seek Him, but God Himself.

We may take a last word on the art of dying well from Henry Suso, in his *Orologium Sapientiæ*:

"That is a sovereign gift of God; soothly for a man to con to die is for to have his heart and his soul at all times upward to those things that be above; that is to say that what time death cometh it find him ready, so that he receive it gladly, without any withdrawing; right as he that bideth the desired coming of his well-beloved fellow."[1]

PRAYER FOR HAPPY DEATH.[2]

Oh, my Lord and Saviour, support me in that hour in the strong arms of Thy Sacraments, and by the fresh fragrance of Thy consolations. Let the absolving words be said over me, and the holy oil sign and seal me, and Thy own Body be my food, and Thy Blood my sprinkling; and let my sweet Mother, Mary, breathe on me, and my Angel whisper peace to me, and my glorious saints . . . smile upon me; that in them all and through them all, I may receive the gift of perseverance, and die, as I desire to live, in Thy faith, in Thy Church, in Thy service, and in Thy love. Amen.

GEORGE CONGREVE, S.S.J.E.

[1] *v.* p. 106.
[2] Cardinal Newman's *Meditations and Devotions*.

INTRODUCTORY NOTE TO THE BOOK

DEATH is the greatest fact in life. It faces us from our earliest consciousness. There is nothing startling in it to the child's mind. As children many of our happiest moments were centred round the funerals of our pet animals.

A wedding or a festival,
A mourning or a funeral;
  And this hath now his heart,
And unto this he frames his tongue.

And it was the same in the childhood of the race. In mediæval times death was a favourite theme. The Mystery plays nearly all ended in heaven or hell, for which there were special pageants; and the influence of these plays is very great on these writings on death. We have only to compare *Everyman*—perhaps the best known of these early plays—with the last tract in this book to see how close is the resemblance. In the latter the Dying Creature summons to his aid reason, dread, conscience, his five wits, faith, hope, charity, and last of all our Lady, by whose aid he is delivered; in *Everyman* when Fellowship, his cousin and his kindred fail him, Good-Deeds brings him to Knowledge, who in turn leads him to Confession. Then his friends gather round him—Discretion, Strength, Five-wits, and Beauty—but only to desert him when they find that his pilgrimage is to the grave. But Knowledge, Good-Deeds, and his Angel remain with him unto the end, and the Doctor draws a moral.

It is worth reading the two together to see how the play has helped to shape the treatise, and yet how much less crude, and finer in thought is the latter.

And that is to be expected, for not only are these treatises of later date, but they were not popular in the sense in which the Plays were popular, but were the grave and thoughtful writings of men of authority and weight, and translated and printed so frequently during the fifteenth and sixteenth centuries that we can only conclude that they were of real service and help. The view of death is the same in both, as was natural. In the Mystery Plays the spiritual life of the soul had to be depicted as a contest for Everyman between his good and evil angels; and at death this struggle, as they thought, was at its fiercest. The death-bed was the great battlefield where man's enemy, the devil, staked his last throw, and drew up all his strongest forces for one final and bitter assault. Every temptation to which the soul had been subjected in the long days of its pilgrimage on earth was now arrayed against it; but against each diabolical temptation was set the Inspiration of the Good Angel, as we see in the pictures of the old block-book.

Since then our whole attitude of mind in regard to

death has changed. Until lately we were inclined to put the thought of death aside as something of which it was not good manners to speak, even in illness. Then more especially the thought of death must be banished. In the old days it was commanded that the leech and physician of the body should give no help to the sick man's body until they had admonished and warned him to take first the spiritual medicine, which the Church has always ready in her keeping. To-day it is not infrequent to meet with those who think it unlucky to send for a priest or minister. "Is he as bad as that?" is the question often asked. With many there is less attempt than there used to be to prepare for death as the last great sacrament of life; the outward sign of a new birth, a second baptism.

But the grim reality of death, which has become to most of us during these three years a household word, a constant companion, has brought back quite simply and naturally many outward signs which for long we have been content without. Calvaries and wayside crosses are again becoming familiar in our streets. Rogation processions are more frequent. Before long may we not hope that other processions also may be restored, even as Mystery Plays are already resuming their old office of teaching the young and the ignorant.

And since we have been made to realise more than ever before the inevitableness of death, is it not well to "learn to die" as this book would teach us? Shall we learn to greet it as a friend for whose coming we have long looked "in thought and desiring" and welcome, when it comes as we should welcome one who rids us of a heavy burden; or shall we dread it because it takes from us that by which we have set most store? Shall we look upon it as the beginning of life, or as the end? "For this death they clepen life, and the death, that these good men (clepen the) beginning of life, they clepen the end."

Or shall it remain to us something which we refuse to think of until we must. Men die none the less bravely for that refusal The spirit of the French Noblesse who met the guillotine with a mocking jest is still with us. We will scorn death as we scorn our enemy.

Perhaps these old writings will at least rouse us to think. They may seem too far remote from our present outlook to be of any practical value. Shelley, dead nearly ninety years ago and yet the most modern of our poets, likens death to sleep, and the scientist to-day would use the same simile. To all appearances we, for the most part, slip out of life unconsciously with little fear, so doctors tell us. As we were born so we die. "The child cries out when from the right breast the mother takes it away, in the very next moment to find in the left one its consolation."

All this seems far removed from the thought of death as a hand to hand conflict of the soul with the powers of evil.

Is it because we have lost sight of the fact that death is far more than a natural process. It is but the outward sign of a much greater reality. The last great sacrament of which we can only partake once; for which all life should be a preparation: And therefore when it comes we do not need to be brave, as in the presence of a foe, but we stretch out our hands in welcome as to a friend we have "long abideth and looked after." "For love is stalworth as death; and love is hard as hades."

And in death we meet the Conqueror of death; we meet Love.

F. M. M. C.

Feast of St Mary Magdalene, 1917

THE BOOK OF THE CRAFT OF DYING

TABLE OF CHAPTERS

HERE BEGINNETH THE BOOK OF THE CRAFT OF DYING

FORASMUCH as the passage of death, of the wretchedness of the exile of this world, for uncunning[1] of dying—not only to lewd men[2] but also to religious and devout persons—seemeth wonderfully hard and perilous, and also right fearful and horrible; therefore in this present matter and treatise, that is of the Craft of Dying, is drawn and contained a short manner of exhortation, for teaching and comforting of them that be in point of death. This manner of exhortation ought subtly to be considered, noted, and understood in the sight of man's soul; for doubtless it is and may be profitable generally, to all true Christian men, to learn and have craft and knowledge to die well.

This matter and treatise containeth six parts of chapters:

The first is of commendation of death; and cunning to die well.

The second containeth the temptations of men that die.

The third containeth the interrogations that should

[1] *i.e.* ignorance. [2] laymen.

be asked of them that be in their death bed, while they may [1] speak and understand.

The fourth containeth an information, with certain obsecrations to them that shall die.

The fifth containeth an instruction to them that shall die.

The sixth containeth prayers that should be said to them that be a-dying, of some men that be about them.

[1] 'may' is generally equivalent to modern 'can.'

CHAPTER I

THE FIRST CHAPTER IS OF COMMENDATION OF DEATH AND OF CUNNING TO[1] DIE WELL

THOUGH bodily death be most dreadful of all fearful things, as the *Philosopher*[2] saith in the third book of Ethics, yet spiritual death of the soul is as much more horrible and detestable, as the soul is more worthy and precious than the body; as the prophet *David* saith: MORS PECCATORUM PESSIMA. The Ps. xxxiii.
death of the sinful man is worst of all deaths. But 22.
as the same prophet saith: PRECIOSA EST IN CONSPECTU Ps. cxv.
DOMINI MORS SANCTORUM EIUS. The death of the 15.
good man is ever precious in the sight of God, what manner of bodily death that ever they die. And thou shalt understand also that not only the death of holy martyrs is so precious, but also the death of all other rightful and good Christian men; and furthermore the death, doubtless, of all sinful men: how long, and how wicked, and how cursed they have been all their life before, unto their last end that they die in—if they die in the state of very[3] repentance and contrition, and in the very faith, and virtue, and

[1] *i.e.* knowing how to.
[2] Aristotle.
[3] Always means 'true,' 'real.'

charity of Holy Church—is acceptable and precious
in the sight of God. As *Saint John* saith in the
Rev. xiv. Apocalypse: BEATI MORTUI QUI IN DOMINO MORI-
13. UNTUR. Blessed be all dead men that die in God.

And therefore God saith in the fourth chapter of
Wis. iv. 7. the Book of Sapience: JUSTUS SI MORTE PRÆOCUPATUS
FUERIT, IN REFRIGERIO ERIT. A rightful man though
he be hasted, or hastily or suddenly dead, he shall
be had to a place of refreshing. And so shall every
man that dieth, if it be so that he keep himself stably,
and govern him wisely in the temptations that he
shall have in [the] agony or strife of his death; as
it shall be declared afterwards. And therefore of
the commendation of death of good men only a
wise man saith thus: Death is nothing else but a
going [out] of prison, and an ending of exile; a
discharging of an heavy burden, that is the body;
finishing of all infirmities; a scaping of all perils;
destroying of all evil things; breaking of all bonds;
paying of [the] debt of natural duty; turning again
into his country; and entering into bliss and joy.

And therefore it is said in the seventh book of
Eccles. *Ecclesiastes*: MELIOR EST DIES MORTIS DIE NATIVITATIS.
vii. 1. The day of man's death is better than the day of
man's birth. And this is understood only of good
men and the chosen people of God. For of evil
men and reprovable, neither the day of their birth,
neither the day of their death, may be called good.
And therefore every good perfect Christian man, and
also every other man though he be imperfect and
late converted from sin, so he be verily contrite and

believe in God, should not be sorry nor troubled, neither dread death of his body, in what manner wise or for what manner cause that he be put thereto; but gladly and wilfully, with reason of his mind that ruleth his sensuality,[1] he should take his death and suffer it patiently, conforming and committing fully his will to God's will and to God's disposition alone, if he will go hence and die well and surely: witnessing the wise man that saith thus: BENE MORI, EST LIBENTER MORI. To die well is to die gladly and wilfully.

And therefore he addeth, and saith thereto: UT SATIS VIXERIM, NEC ANNI, NEC DIES FACIUNT, SED ANIMUS. Neither many days, nor many years, cause me to say and feel that I have lived long [enough,] but only the reasonable will of mine heart and of my soul. Sith more than that, of duty and natural right all men must needly die;[2] and that how, when, and where that Almighty God will; and God's will is evermore good, and over all good, in all things good, and just, and rightful. For as *John Cassian* saith in his *Collations*: Almighty God of His wisdom and Collat. goodness, all things that fall, both prosperity and i. 5. adversity, disposeth ever finally for our profit, and for the best for us; and more provideth, and is busier for the heal and salvation of His chosen children, than we ourselves may or can be.

And sith, as it is aforesaid, we may not, in no wise, neither flee nor escape, neither change the

[1] *i.e.* his bodily nature.

[2] *Cum igitur ex debito atque jure naturali omnes homines mori sit necesse.*

inevitable necessity and passage of death, therefore we ought to take our death when God will, wilfully and gladly, without any grutching [1] or contradiction, through the might and boldness of the will of our soul virtuously disposed and governed by reason and very discretion; though the lewd [2] sensuality and frailty of our flesh naturally grutch or strive there against. And therefore *Seneca* saith thus: FERAS, NON CULPES, QUOD IMMUTARE NON VALES. Suffer easily and blame thou not, that thou mayst not change nor void. And the same clerk added to, and saith: SI VIS ISTA CUM QUIBUS URGERIS EFFUGERE, NON UT ALIBI SIS OPORTEAT, SED ALIUS. If thou wilt escape that thou art straitly be-wrapped [3] in, it needeth not that thou be in another place, but that thou be another man.

Furthermore, that a Christian man may die well and seemly,[4] him needeth that he con [5] die, and as a wise man saith: SCIRE MORI EST PARATUM COR SUUM HABERE, ET ANIMAM AD SUPERNA: UT QUANDOCUNQUE MORS ADVENERIT, PARATUM CUM INVENIAT UT ABSQUE OMNI RETRACTIONE EAM RECIPIAT, QUASI QUI SOCII SUI DILECTI ADVENTUM DESIDERATUM EXPECTAT. To con die is to have an heart and a soul every ready up to Godward, that when-that-ever death come, he may be found all ready; withouten any retraction [6] receive him, as a man would

[1] murmuring.
[2] evil.
[3] The other MSS. have 'trapped.'
[4] The other MSS. have 'surely.'
[5] learn to.
[6] *i.e.* withdrawal.

receive his well-beloved and trusty friend and fellow, that he had long abideth and looked after.

This cunning is most profitable of all cunnings, in the which cunning religious men specially, more than other, and every day continually, should study more diligently than other men that they might apprehend it; namely[1] for the state of religion asketh and requireth it more in them than in others. Notwithstanding that every secular man, both clerk and layman, whether he be disposed and ready to die or no, yet nevertheless he must needs die when God will. Therefore ought every man, not only religious, but also every good and devout Christian man that desireth for to die well and surely, live in such wise and so have himself alway, that he may safely die, every hour, when God will. And so he should have his life in patience, and his death in desire, as *Saint Paul* had when he said: CUPIO Philip. i.
DISSOLVI ET ESSE CUM CHRISTO. I desire and covet 23.
to be dead, and be with Christ. And thus much sufficeth at this time, shortly said, of [the] craft and science of dying.

CHAPTER II

THE SECOND CHAPTER IS OF MEN'S TEMPTATIONS THAT DIE

KNOW all men doubtless, that men that die, in their last sickness and end, have greatest and most grievous

[1] 'namely' generally means (as here) 'especially,' 'chiefly.'

temptations, and such as they never had before in all their life. And of these temptations five be most principal.

I. The First is of the faith, forasmuch as faith is fundament of all men's soul's-heal; witnessing 1 Cor. iii. 11. the Apostle that saith: Fundamentum aliud nemo potest ponere. Other fundament may no man put. And therefore *Saint Austin* saith: Fides est bonorum omnium fundamentum, et humane salutis initium. Faith is fundament of all goodness, and beginning Heb. xi. 6. of man's heal. And therefore saith *Saint Paul*: Sine fide est impossibile placere Deo. It is impossible to please God without faith. And *Saint Austin* saith: Qui non credit jam judicatus est. He that believeth not is now deemed. And forasmuch as there is such and so great strength in the faith that withouten it there may no man be saved.

Therefore the devil with all his might is busy to avert fully a man from the faith in his last end; or, if he may not, that he laboureth busily to make his doubt therein, or somewhat draw him out of the way or deceive him with some manner of superstitious and false errors or heresies. But every good Christian man is bound namely habitually, though he may not actually and intellectually apprehend them, to believe, and full faith and credence give, not only to the principal articles of the faith, but also to all holy writ in all manner things; and fully to obey the statutes of the church of Rome, and stably to abide and die in them. For as soon as he beginneth to err or doubt in any of them all, as soon he goeth out of the way of life, and his soul's heal. But wit thou well without doubt, that in this temptation, and in all other that follow after, the devil may not noy thee, nor prevail against no man, in no wise, as long as he hath use of his free will, and of reason well disposed, but if[1] he will wilfully consent unto his temptation.

And therefore no very Christian[2] man ought (not) to dread any of his illusions, or his false threatenings,[3] or his feigned fearings. For as Christ himself saith in the gospel: DIABOLUS EST MENDAX ET PATER EIUS. The devil is a liar, and a father of all leasings. But manly, therefore, and stiffly and steadfastly abide and persevere; and die in the very faith and unity and obedience of our mother Holy Church.

S. John viii. 44.

And it is right profitable and good, as it is used in some religious, when a man is in agony of dying, with an high voice oft times to say the Creed before him, that he that is sick may be mortified in stableness of the faith; and fiends that may not suffer to hear it may be voided and driven away from him. Also to stableness of very faith should strengthen a sick man principally the stable faith of our holy Fathers, Abraham, Isaac, and Jacob. Also the perseverant abiding faith of Job, of Raab the woman, and Achor, and such other. And also the faith of the Apostles, and other martyrs, confessors, and virgins innumerable.

[1] Always means 'unless.'
[2] *bonus Catholicus Christianus.*
[3] The other MSS. have 'persuasions.'

For by faith all they that have been of old time before us—and all they be now and shall be hereafter—they all please, and have [pleased] and shall please God by faith. For as it is aforesaid: Withouten faith it is impossible to please God.

Also double profit should induce every sick man to be stable in faith. One is: For faith may do all things; as our Lord Himself witnesseth in the gospel, and saith: OMNIA POSSIBILIA SUNT CREDENTI. All things are possible to him that believeth steadfastly. Another is: For faith getteth a man all things. As our Lord saith: QUICQUID ORANTES PETITIS, CREDITE QUIA ACCIPIETIS, ET FIET VOBIS, etc. Whatever it be that ye will pray and ask, believe verily that [ye] shall take[1] it, and ye shall have it; though that ye would say to an hill that he should lift himself up and fall into the sea, as the hills of Capsye by prayer and petition of King Alexander, the great conqueror, were closed together.

S. Mark ix. 22.

S. Mark xi. 24.

II. The Second Temptation is Desperation; the which is against [the] hope and confidence that every man should have unto God. For when a sick man is sore tormented and vexed, with sorrow and sickness of his body, then the devil is most busy to superadd sorrow to sorrow, with all [the] ways that he may, objecting his sins against him for to induce him into despair.

De vilitate cond. hum. lib. 3.

Furthermore as *Innocent* the Pope, in his third book of the wickedness of mankind, saith: Every man both good and evil, or[2] his soul pass out of his

[1] *i.e.* receive. [2] before.

body, he seeth Christ put on the cross: the good man to his consolation, the evil man to his confusion, to make him ashamed that he hath lost the fruit of his redemption.

Also the devil bringeth again into a man's mind that is in point of death specially those sins that he hath done, and was not shriven of, to draw him thereby into despair. But therefore should no man despair in no wise. For though any one man or woman had done as many thefts, or manslaughters, or as many other sins as be drops of water in the sea, and gravel stones in the strand, though he had never done penance for them afore, nor never had been shriven of them before—neither then might have time, for sickness or lack of speech, or shortness of time, to be shriven of them—yet should he never despair; for in such a case very contrition of heart within, with will to be shriven if time sufficed, is sufficient and accepted by God for to save him everlastingly: as the Prophet saith in the psalm: COR CONTRITUM ET HUMILITATUM, DEUS, NON DESPICIES. Lord God, Thou wilt never despise a contrite heart and a meek. And *Ezechiel* saith also: IN QUACUNQUE HORA CONVERSUS FUERIT PECCATOR, ET INGEMUERIT, SALVUS ERIT. In what hour that ever it be that the sinful man is sorry inward, and converted from his sins, he shall be saved.

Ps. l. 19.

Ezech. xxxiii. 12.

And therefore *Saint Bernard* saith: The pity and mercy of God is more than any wickedness. And *Austin*, upon John, saith: We should never despair of no man as long as he is in his bodily life, for there is no sin so great but it may be healed, outake[1] despair alone. And *Saint Austin* saith also : All sins that a man hath done afore may not noy nor damn a man, but if he be well payd[2] in his heart that he hath done them. Therefore no man should despair, though it were so that it were possible that he alone had done all manner of sins that might be done in the world. For by despair a man getteth nought else but that God is much more offended thereby ; and all his other sins be more grievous[3] in God's sight, and everlasting pain thereby increased infinitely to him that so despaireth.

Therefore against despair, for to induce him that is sick and laboureth in his dying to very trust and confidence that he should principally have to God at that time, the disposition of Christ in the cross should greatly draw him. Of the which *Saint Bernard* saith thus : What man is he that should not be ravished and drawn to hope, and have full confidence in God, and he take heed diligently of the disposition of Christ's body in the cross. Take heed and see : His head is inclined to salve thee ; His mouth to kiss thee ; His arms spread to be-clip[4] thee ; His hands thrilled[5] to give thee ; His side opened to love thee ; His body along strait to give all Himself to thee.

Therefore no man should despair of forgiveness, but fully have hope and confidence in God ; for the virtue of hope is greatly commendable, and of great

[1] *i.e.* except.
[2] pleased.
[3] The other MSS. have 'augmented.'
[4] embrace.
[5] pierced.

merit before God. As the Apostle saith, and exhorted us: NOLITE AMITTERE CONFIDENTIAM VESTRAM QUÆ MAGNAM HABET REMUNERATIONEM. Lose not your hope and confidence in God, the which hath great reward of God. Heb. v. 35.

Furthermore, that no sinful man should in no wise despair—have he sinned never so greatly, nor never so sore, nor never so oft, nor never so long continued therein—we have open ensample in Peter that denied Christ; in Paul that pursued Holy Church; in Matthew and Zaccheus, the publicans; in Mary Maudeleyn, the sinful woman, [in the woman [1]] that was taken in avoutry; in the thief that hung on the cross beside Christ; in Mary Egyptian; and in innumerable other grievous and great sinners.

III. The Third Temptation is Impatience; the which is against charity, by the which we be bound to love God above all things. For they that be in sickness, in their death bed suffer passingly [2] great pain and sorrow and woe; and namely they that die not by nature and course of age—that happeth right seldom, as open experience teacheth men—but die often through an accidental sickness; as a fever, a postune,[3] and such other grievous and painful and long sickness. The which many men, and namely those that be undisposed [4] to die and die against their will and lack very charity, maketh so impatient and grutching, that other while,[5] through woe and im-

[1] Insertions in square brackets, here and elsewhere, are from the Douce MS. (D).
[2] *i.e.* surpassingly.
[3] tumour.
[4] unprepared.
[5] at times.

patience, they become wood [1] and witless, as it hath been seen in many men. And so by that it is open and certain that they that die in that wise fail and lack very charity. Witnessing *Saint Jerome*, that saith thus: SI QUIS CUM DOLORE EGRITUDINEM VEL MORTEM SUSCEPERIT, SIGNUM EST QUOD DEUS SUFFICIENTER NON DILIGIT. That is: Whoso taketh sickness or death with sorrow or displeasure of heart, it is an open and a certain sign that he loveth not God sufficiently. Therefore that man that will die well, it is needful that he grutch not in no manner of sickness that falleth to him before his death, or in his dying—be it never so painful or grievous—long time [or short time] dying; for as *Saint Gregory* witnesseth in his *Morals*: JUSTA SUNT CUNCTA QUE PATIMUR, ET IDEO VALDE INJUSTUM EST SI DE JUSTA PASSIONE MURMURAMUS. All things that we suffer, we suffer then rightfully [and therefore we be greatly unrightful if we grutch
S. Luke of that we suffer rightfully]. Then every man should
xxi. 19. be patient, as *Saint Luke* saith: IN PATIENTIA VESTRA POSSIDEBITIS ANIMAS VESTRAS. In your patience ye shall possess [2] your souls. For by patience man's soul is surely had and kept, so by impatience and murmuration it is lost and damned. Witnessing *Saint Gregory* in his Homily, that saith thus: REGNUM CŒLORUM NULLUS MURMURANS ACCIPIT, NULLUS QUI ACCIPIT MURMURARE POTEST. There shall no man have the kingdom of heaven that grutcheth and is impatient; and there may no man grutch that hath it. But as the great Clerk *Albert* saith, speaking of very

[1] mad. [2] D. 'welde.'

contrition: If a very contrite man offereth himself gladly to all manner afflictions of sickness and punishing of his sins, that he may thereby satisfy God worthily for his offences, much more then every sick man should suffer patiently and gladly his own sickness alone, that is lighter without comparison than many sicknesses that other men suffer; namely[1] that sickness before a man's death is as a purgatory to him, when it is suffered as it ought; that is to understand, if it be suffered patiently, gladly, and with a free and a kind will of heart. For the same clerk *Albert* saith: We have need to have a free, kind will to God, not only in such things as be to our consolation, but also in such things as be to our affliction. And *Saint Gregory* saith: DIVINA DISPENSATIONE AGITUR, UT PROLIXIORI VICIO PROLIXIOR EGRITUDO ADHIBEATUR. It is done by the disposition and rightful ordinance of God that to the longer sin is ordained the longer sickness. And therefore let every sick man, and namely he that shall die, say as *Saint Austin* said to God: HIC SECA, HIS URE, UT IN ETERNAM MICHI PARCAS. Here cut, here burn, so that Thou spare me everlastingly. And *Saint Gregory* saith: MISERICORS DEUS TEMPORALEM ADHIBET SEVERITATEM, NE ETERNAM INFERAT ULTIONEM. God that is merciful giveth His chosen children temporal punition here, lest He give them everlasting vengeance elsewhere.

This temptation of impatience fighteth against charity, and without charity may no men be saved. And therefore, as *Saint Paul* saith: CARITAS PACIENS 1 Cor. xiii. 4.

[1] The other MSS. have 'sithen.'

EST, OMNIA SUFFERT. Very charity is patient, and suffereth all things. And in these words it is notable to be marked that he spake of suffering of all things, and outake[1] nothing. Then should all sicknesses of the body by reason be suffered patiently, without murmuration and difficulty. And therefore, as *Saint Austin* saith: AMANTI NICHIL IMPOSSIBILE, NICHIL DIFFICILE. To him that loveth there is nothing hard, nor nothing impossible.

IV. The Fourth Temptation is Complacence, or pleasance of a man that he hath in himself; that is spiritual pride, with the which the devil tempteth and beguileth most religious, and devout and perfect men. For when the devil seeth that he may not bring a man out of faith, nor may not induce him into despair, neither to impatience, then he assaileth him by complacence of himself, putting such manner temptations in his heart: O how stable art thou in the faith! how strong in hope! how sad in patience! O how many good deeds hast thou done! and such other thoughts. But against these temptations *Isidore* saith thus: NON TE ARROGES, NON TE JACTES, NON TE INSOLENTER EXTOLLAS, VEL DE TE PRESUMAS, NICHIL BONI TIBI TRIBUAS. Nor boast thou not, nor avaunt thee not proudly, not make not much of thyself wantonly, nor arret[2] not goodness to thy self; for a man may have so much delectation in such manner of complacence of himself that a man should be damned everlastingly therefore.

And therefore saith *Saint Gregory*: QUIS REMINISC-

[1] *i.e.* excepts. [2] ascribe.

ENDO BONA QUE GESSIT, DUM SE APUD SE ERIGIT, APUD AUCTOREM HUMILITATIS CADIT. A man that thinketh on (the) good deeds that he hath done, and is proud thereof of himself within himself, he falleth down anon [1] before Him that is author of meekness. And therefore he that shall die must beware when he feeleth himself tempted with pride, that then he [low and] meek himself thinking on his sins: and that he wot never whether he be worthy everlasting love or hate, that is to say, salvation or damnation. Nevertheless, lest he despair, he must lift up his heart to God by hope, thinking and revolving [2] stably that the mercy of God is above all His works, and that God is true in all His words, and that He is truth and righteousness that never beguileth, neither is beguiled, which be-hight [3] and swore by Himself, and said by the Prophet: VIVO EGO, DICIT DOMINUS, NOLO MORTEM Ezech.
PECCATORIS, etc. God Almighty saith: By my self I xxxiii. 11.
will not the death neither the damnation of no sinful man, but that he convert himself to Me and be saved. Every man should follow *Saint Antony* to whom the devil said: Antony, thou hast overcome me; for when I would have thee up by pride, thou keptest thyself a-down by meekness; and when I would draw thee down by desperation, thou keptest thyself up by hope. Thus should every man do, sick and whole, and then is the devil overcome.

V. The Fifth [Temptation] that tempteth and grieveth most carnal men and secular men, that be in

[1] *i.e.* at once, immediately.
[2] The other MSS. have 'remembering.' [3] vowed.

overmuch occupation, and business outward about temporal things; that is their wives, their children, their carnal friends, and their worldly riches, and other things that they have loved inordinately before. For he that will die well and surely must utterly and fully put away out of his mind all temporal and outward things, and plenerly[1] commit himself all to God. And therefore the great clerk *Dons* [*Scotus*] saith thus, in the fourth book of sentences: What man that is sick, when he seeth that he shall die, if he put his will thereto to die wilfully, and consenteth fully unto death, as though he hath chose himself the pain of death voluntarily, and so suffereth death patiently, he satisfieth to God for all venial sins; and therefore[2] he taketh away a parcel of satisfaction that he ought to do for deadly sins. And therefore it is right profitable, and full necessary in such a point of need, that a man conform his will to God's will in all things, as every man ought, both sick and whole. But it is seldom seen that any secular or carnal man—or religious either—will dispose himself to death; or furthermore, that is worse, will hear anything of the matter of death; [though indeed he be labouring fast to his endward, hoping that he shall escape the death and] that is the most perilous thing, and most inconvenient that may be in Christian man, as saith the worthy clerk *Cantor Pariensis*:[3]

But it is to be noted well that the devil in all these temptations abovesaid may compel no man, nor in no

[1] fully. [2] The other MSS. have 'furthermore.'
[3] Petrus Cantor Paris (d. 1197. Opp. in Migne, vol. 205).

manner of wise prevail against him for to consent to him—as long as a man hath the use of reason with him—but if he will wilfully consent unto him ; that every good Christian man, and also every sinful man—be he never so great a sinner—ought to beware of above all things. For the Apostle saith : FIDELIS DEUS QUI NON PATIETUR VOS TEMPTARI SUPRA ID QUOD POTESTIS, SED FACIET ETIAM CUM TEMPTATIONE PROVENTUM UT POSSITIS SUSTINERE. God, he saith, is true, and will not suffer you to be tempted more than ye may bear ; but He will give you such support in your temptations that ye may bear them. 1 Cor. x. 13.

Whereupon saith the gloss : God is true in His promises, and giveth us grace to withstand mightily, manly, and perseverantly ; giving us might that we be not overcome, grace to get us merit, steadfastness to overcome with. He giveth such increase of virtue that we may suffer and not fail nor fall ; and that is by meekness. For as *Saint Austin* saith : They break not in the furnace that have not the wind of pride. Therefore (let) every man, rightful and sinful, bow himself, and submit himself fully unto the mighty hand of God ; and with His help he shall surely get and have the victory in all manner of temptations, evils, and sorrows, and of death thereto.

CHAPTER III

THE THIRD CHAPTER CONTAINETH THE INTERROGATIONS THAT SHOULD BE ASKED OF THEM THAT BE IN THEIR DEATH BED, WHILE THEY MAY SPEAK AND UNDERSTAND

Now follow the interrogations of them that draw to the death, while they have reason with them and their speech. For this cause if any man is not fully disposed to die, he may the better be informed and comforted [thereto]. And as *Saint Anselm* the bishop saith and teacheth, these interrogations should be had unto them that be in that plight.

First ask him this:

Brother, art thou glad that thou shalt die in the faith of Christ? The sick man answereth: Yea.

Knowest thou well that thou hast not done as thou shouldst have done? He answereth: Yea.

Repentest thee thereof? He answereth: Yea.

Hast thou full will to amend thee, if thou mightest have full space of life? He answereth: Yea.

Believest thou fully that Our Lord Jesu Christ, God's Son, died for thee? He sayeth: Yea.

Thankest thou Him thereof with all thine heart? He answereth: Yea.

Believest thou verily that thou mayest not be saved but by Christ's [death and His] passion? He answereth: Yea.

Then thank Him thereof ever, while thy soul is in thy body, and put all thy trust in His passion and in His death only, having trust in none other thing. To this death commit thee fully.[1] In His death wrap all thyself fully; and if it come to thy mind, or by thine enemy it be put into thy mind, that God will deem thee, say thus:

LORD, I put the death of Our Lord Jesu Christ between me and mine evil deeds, between me and the judgment; otherwise will I not strive with Thee.

If He say: Thou hast deserved damnation; say thou again: The death of our Lord Jesu Christ I put between me and mine evil merits, and the merits of His worthy passion I offer for merits I should have had, and alas I have not. Say also: Lord, put the death of my Lord Jesu Christ between me and Thy righteousness.

Then let him say this thrice, IN MANUS TUAS, DOMINE, etc. Into thine hands, Lord, I commit my soul. And let the covent[2] say the same. And if he may not speak, let the covent—or they that stand about—say thus: IN MANUS TUAS, DOMINE, COMMENDAMUS SPIRITUM EIUS, etc. Into Thine hands, Lord, we commend his soul. And thus he dieth surely; and he shall not die everlastingly.

But though these interrogations abovesaid be com-

[1] The other MSS. have 'with His death cover thee fully.'
[2] *i.e.* convent.

petent and sufficient to religious and devout persons, nevertheless all Christian men, both secular and religious, after the doctrines of the noble Clerk the *Chancellor of Paris*, in their last end should be examined, enquired, and informed, more certainly and clearly, of the state and the health of their souls.

I. And First thus: Believest thou fully all the principal articles of the faith; and also all Holy Scripture in all things, after the exposition of the holy and true doctors of Holy Church; and forsakest all heresies and errors and opinions damned by the Church; and art glad also that thou shalt die in the faith of Christ, and in the unity and obedience of Holy Church?

The sick man answering: Yea.

II. The Second Interrogation shall be this: Knowledgest thou that often times, and in many manner wises, and grievously, thou hast offended thy Lord God that made thee of nought? For *Saint Bernard* saith upon CANTICA CANTICORUM: I know well that there may no man be saved but if he know himself; of which knowing waxeth in a man humility, that is the mother of his health, and also the dread of God, the which dread, as it is the beginning of wisdom, so it is the beginning of health of man's soul.

He answereth: Yea.

III. The Third Interrogation shall be this: Art thou sorry in heart of all manner of sins that thou hast done against the high Majesty, and the Love of God, and the Goodness of God; and of all the goodness that thou hast not done, and mightest have done; and of all graces that thou hast slothed[1]—not only for dread of death, or any other pain, but rather[2] more for love of God and His righteousness—and for thou hast displeased His great goodness and kindness; and for the due order of charity, by the which we be bound to love God above all things; and of all these things thou askest the forgiveness of God? Desirest thou also in thine heart to have very knowing of all thine offences and forgets that thou hast done against God, and to have special repentance of them all?[3]

He answereth: Yea.

IV. The Fourth Interrogation shall be this: Purposeth thou verily, and art in full will, to amend thee if thou mightest live longer; and never to sin more, deadly, wittingly, and with thy will: and rather than thou wouldest offend God deadly any more, to leave and lose wilfully all earthly things, were they never so lief to thee, and also the life of thy body thereto? And furthermore thou prayest God that He give thee grace to continue in this purpose?

He answereth: Yea.

V. The Fifth Interrogation shall be this: Forgivest thou fully in thine heart all manner men that ever have done thee any manner harm or grievance unto this time, either in word or in deed, for the

[1] *i.e.* delayed, neglected. [2] *i.e.* sooner.

[3] *Optas insuper cor tuum illuminari ad oblitorum cognitionem ut de eis specialiter valeas penitere.*

love and worship of Our Lord Jesu Christ, of Whom thou hopest of forgiveness thyself; and askest also thyself to have forgiveness of all [them thou hast offended in any] manner wise?

He answereth: Yea.

VI. The Sixth Interrogation shall be this: Wilt thou that all manner things that thou hast in any manner wise misgotten, be fully restored again,—so much as thou mayst, and art bound, after the value of thy goods; and rather leave and forsake all the goods of the world, if thou mayst not in none other wise?

He answereth: Yea.

VII. The Seventh Interrogation shall be this: Believest thou fully that Christ died for thee, and that thou mayst never be saved but by the mercy of Christ's passion; and thankest thou God thereof with all thine heart, as much as thou mayst?

He answereth: Yea.

Whoso may verily, of very good conscience and truth, withouten any feigning, answer yea to the foresaid seven interrogations, he hath an evident argument enough of health of his soul, that, and he died so, he shall be of the number of them that shall be saved.

Whosoever is not asked of another of these seven interrogations when he is in such peril of death—for there be right few that have the cunning of this craft of dying—he must remember himself in his soul, and ask himself, and subtly feel and consider, whether he be so disposed as it is above said, or no.

For without that a man be disposed in such wise finally, he may not doubtless[1] be saved everlastingly.

And what man that is disposed as is abovesaid, let him commend and commit himself, all in fear, fully to the passion of Christ; and continually—as much as he may, and as his sickness will suffer him—think on the passion of Christ; for thereby all the devil's temptations and guiles be most overcome and voided.

CHAPTER IV

THE FOURTH CHAPTER CONTAINETH AN INSTRUCTION: WITH CERTAIN OBSECRATIONS[2] TO THEM THAT SHALL DIE

FURTHERMORE, forasmuch as *Saint Gregory* saith: Every doing of Christ is our instruction and teaching; therefore such things as Christ did dying on the cross, the same should every man do at his last end, after his cunning[3] and power. And Christ did five things on the cross. He prayed, for He said
these psalms: DEUS, DEUS MEUS, RESPICE IN ME; and Ps xxiv
all the psalms following unto that verse: IN MANUS 16.
TUAS, DOMINE. Also He cried on the cross, as the Ps xxx
apostle witnesseth. Also He wept on the cross. Also 6.
He committed His soul to the Father on the cross. Also wilfully He gave up the ghost on the cross.

First He prayed on the cross. So a sick man, that is in point of death, he should pray; namely in his heart, if he may not with his mouth. For

[1] *i.e.* without doubt, certainly.
[2] supplications.
[3] knowledge.

Saint Isidore saith: That it is better to pray still in the heart, without any sound of voice outward, than to pray with word alone, without devotion of heart.

The second was He cried. So should every man in his dying cry strongly with the heart, not with the voice. For God taketh more heed of the desire of the heart than of the crying of the voice. The crying of the heart to God is nought else but the great desiring of man to have forgiveness of his sins, and to have everlasting life.

The third was He wept. With His bodily eyes and with tears of the heart, in token that so should every man in His dying weep with tears of his heart, that is to say, verily repenting of all his misdeeds.

The fourth He commendeth His soul to God. So should every man in his end, saying thus in heart and mouth, if he may, and (if not) else in heart: Lord God, into Thine hands I commend my spirit; for truly Thou boughtest me dear.

The fifth was He gave up wilfully His spirit. So should every man in his death; that is to say, he should die wilfully, conforming fully therein his own will to God's will, as he is bound.

Therefore as long as he that is in point of death may speak, and have the use of reason with him, let him say these prayers following:

ORATIO

O THOU HIGH GODHEAD, and endless Goodness, most merciful and glorious Trinity, that art highest Love and Charity; have mercy on me, wretched and sinful man, for to Thee I commend fully my soul.

ORATIO

My Lord God, most benign Father of mercy, do Thy mercy to me Thy poor creature. Help now Lord my needy and desolate soul in her last need, that hell hounds devour me not. Most sweetest and most lovely Lord, my Lord Jesu Christ, God's own dear Son, for the worship and the virtue of Thy most blessed passion, admit and receive me within the number of Thy chosen people. My Saviour and my Redemptor, I yield all myself fully unto Thy grace and mercy, forsake me not; to Thee Lord I come, put me not away. Lord Jesu Christ, I ask Thy paradise and bliss, not for the worthiness of my deserving that am but dust and ashes and a sinful wretch, but through the virtue and effect of Thine holy passion, by the which Thou vouchest safe, and wouldest buy me, sinful wretch, with Thy precious blood, and bring me into Thy paradise.

And let him say often also this verse: Dirupisti Domine vincula mea, tibi sacrificabo hostiam laudis et nomen Domini invocabo. Lord Thou hast broken my bonds, and therefore I shall thank Thee with the sacrifice and the oblation of worship. For this verse, as *Cassiodorus* saith, is of great virtue that a man's sins be forgiven him, if it be said thrice with good true faith at a man's last end.

ORATIO

LORD JESUS CHRIST, for the bitterness that Thou sufferedest for me on the cross, and most in that hour when Thy most blessed soul passed out of Thy body, have mercy on my soul in her strait passing.

Also afterward, with all the instance and devotion that he may, with heart and mouth let him cry to Our Lady, Saint Mary, that is most speedful, and most remedious speed and help of all sinful men to God, saying thus :

ORATIO

O GLORIOUS QUEEN OF HEAVEN, Mother of mercy, and refuge of all sinful men ; reconcile me to thy sweet Son, my Lord Jesu, and pray for me sinful wretch, to His great mercy, that for love of thee, sweet Lady, He will forgive me my sins.

Then let him pray to angels, saying thus :

HOLY ANGELS OF HEAVEN, I beseech you that ye will assist to me that shall now pass out of this world, and mightily deliver me and keep me from all mine enemies, and take my soul into your blessed company ; and namely thou my good angel, that hast been my continual keeper, ordained of God.

Then let him pray the same wise, devoutly, to all the apostles, martyrs, and confessors, and virgins—and specially to those saints which he loved and worshipped most specially in his heal—that they would help him then in his last end and most need. Afterwards let him say thrice, or more, these words, or like in sentence,[1] the which be ascribed unto *Saint Austin* :

> THE PEACE OF OUR LORD JESUS CHRIST ; and the virtue of His passion ; and the sign of the holy cross ; and the maidenhead of Our Lady, Saint Mary ; and the blessing of all Saints ; and the keeping of all Angels ; and the suffrages of all the chosen people of God ; be between me and mine enemies, visible and invisible, in this hour of my death. Amen.

Afterward let him say this verse :

> LARGIRE CLARUM VESPERE
> QUO VITA NUSQUAM DECIDAT,
> SED PRÆMIUM MORTIS SACRE,
> PERENNIS INSTET GLORIA.

Grant me Lord a clear end, that my soul fall never downwards ; but give me everlasting bliss, that is the reward of holy dying.

And if he that is sick can not [2] all these prayers, or may not say them for grievousness or sickness, let some man that is about him say them before him, as he may clearly hear him say them, changing the words that ought to be changed in his saying. And he that is dying, as long as he hath use of reason, let him pray devoutly within himself, with his heart and his desire, as he can and may, and so yield the ghost up to God ; and he shall be safe.

[1] meaning. [2] *i.e.*, knows not.

CHAPTER V

THE FIFTH CHAPTER CONTAINETH AN INSTRUCTION UNTO THEM THAT SHALL DIE

But it is greatly to be noted, and to be taken heed of, that right seldom (that) any man—yea among religious and devout men—dispose themselves to death betimes as they ought. For every man weeneth himself to live long, and troweth not that he shall die in short time; and doubtless that cometh of the devil's subtle temptation. And often times it is seen openly that many men, through such idle hope and trust, have for-slothed themselves,[1] and have died intestate, or unavised, or undisposed,[2] suddenly. And therefore every man that hath love and dread of God, and a zeal of [the heal of] man's soul, let him busily induce and warn every of his even christians that is sick, or in any peril of body or of soul, that principally and first, over all other things, and withouten delays and long tarryings, he diligently provide and ordain for the spiritual remedy and medicine of his soul.

[Gratian] *De penitentia.* "*Cum infirmitate.*"

For often times, as a certain decretal saith, bodily sickness cometh of the sickness of the soul; and therefore the Pope in the same decretal chargeth straitly every bodily leech that he give no sick man no bodily medicine unto the time that he hath warned and induced him to seek his spiritual leech.

[1] *i.e.* lost themselves through sloth. [2] *i.e.* unprepared.

But this counsel is now for-slothed almost of all men, and is turned into the contrary; for men seek sooner and busier after medicines for the body than for the soul. Also all our evils and adversities, by righteous doom of God, cometh evermore to men for sins; as the Prophet witnesseth, that saith thus: NON EST MALUM IN CIVITATE, QUOD DEUS NON FECIT. There is none evil in the city, but God do it. Thou shalt not understand that God doeth the evil of the sin, but yieldeth the punishing for sin.

Therefore every sick man, and every other man that is in any peril, should be diligently induced and exhorted that he maketh himself, before all other things, peace with God; receiving spiritual medicines, that is to say the sacraments of Holy Church; ordaining and making his testament; and lawfully disposing for his household, and other needs, if he hath any to dispose for. And there should not be given first to no man too much hope of bodily heal. But the contrary thereof is now often times done of many men, into great peril of souls; and namely of them that actually and openly be drawing and in point hastily to die, for none of them will hear nothing of death.

And so as the great CLERK, the *Chancellor of Paris* saith: Often times by such a [vain and a] false cheering and comforting, and feigned behoting[1] of bodily heal, and trusting thereupon, men run and fall into certain damnation everlastingly. And therefore a sick man should be counselled and ex-

[1] promising.

horted to provide and procure himself his soul's heal by very contrition and confession—and if it be expedient for him, that shall greatly avail to his bodily heal; and so he shall be most quiet and sure.

And forasmuch, witnessing *Saint Gregory*, as a man hath seldom very contrition, and as *Saint Austin* saith also, in the fourth Book of Sentences, the twentieth distinction, and other doctors also: Repentance that is deferred, and had in a man's last end, unneth [1] is very repentance or penance sufficient to everlasting heal. And specially in them that all their time before neither the commandments of God nor their voluntary avows kept not effectually nor truly, but only feignedly and to the outward seeming.

Therefore to every such man that is in such case and is come to his last end, is to be counselled busily that he labour, with reason of his mind after his power, to have ordinate and very repentance; that is to mean—notwithstanding the sorrow and grievance of sickness, and dread that he hath of hasty death—that he use reason as much as he may, and enforce himself to have, wilfully, full displeasing of all sin, for the due end and perfect intent that is for God; and withstand his evil natural inclining to sin, though he might live longer, and also the delectations of his sins before; and labour as much as he may to have a very displeasure of them, though it be never so short. And lest he fall into despair tell him, and arm him with

[1] seldom.

such things as be said above, in the second part, of temptation of Desperation. Exhort him also that he be strong in his soul against other temptations that be put and told, also mightily and manly withstand them all; for he may not be compelled by the devil to consent to none of them all. Let him also be charged[1] and counselled that he die as a very true Christian man, and in full belief.

Also it is to be considered whether he be involved with any censures of Holy Church; and if he be let him be taught that he submit himself with all his might to the ordinance of Holy Church, that he may be assoiled. Also, if he that shall die have long time and space to be-think himself, and be not taken with hasty death, then may be read afore him, of them that be about him, devout histories and devout prayers, in the which he most delighted in when he was in heal; or rehearse to him the commandments of God, that he may be-think him the more profoundly if he may find in himself that he hath negligently trespassed against them.

And if the sick man hath lost his speech, and yet he hath full knowledge of the interrogations that be made to him, or the prayers that be rehearsed before him, then only with some outer sign, or with consent of heart, let him answer thereto. Nevertheless it is greatly to be charged and hasted[2] that the interrogations be made to him or he lose his speech; for if his answers be not likely, and seemeth not in all sides to be sufficient to full heal and perpetual remedy of his

[1] The other MSS. have 'monished.' [2] *i.e.* urged.

soul, then must he put thereto remedy and counsel in the best manner that it may be done.

Then there shall be told unto him plainly the peril that he should fall in, though he should and would be greatly a-feared thereof. It is better and more rightful that he be compunctious and repentant, with wholesome fear and dread, and so be saved, than that he be damned with flattering and false dissimulation; for it is too inconvenient[1] and contrary to Christian religion, and too devil-like, that the peril of death and of soul—for any vain dread of a man, lest he were anything distroubled thereby—shall be hid from any Christian man or woman that should die. But *Isaye the Prophet* did the contrary; for when the King Ezechiel lay sick and upon the point of death, he glosed[2] him not, nor used no dissimulation unto him, but plainly and wholesomely a-ghasted him,[3] saying that he should die; and yet nevertheless he died not at that time. And *Saint Gregory* also wholesomely a-ghasted the monk that was approprietary,[4] as it is read in the fourth Book of his Dialogues.

Also present to the sick the image of the crucifix; the which should evermore be about sick men, or else the image of our Lady, or of some other saint the which he loved or worshipped in his heal. Also let there be holy water about the sick; and spring[5] often times upon him, and the others that be about him, that fiends may be voided from him.

[1] inconsistent. [2] flattered. [3] *i.e.* frightened him.
[4] *i.e.* who had appropriated what belonged to another.
[5] sprinkle.

If all things abovesaid may not be done, for hastiness [1] and shortness of time, then put forth prayers; and namely such as be directed to our Saviour, specially Our Lord Jesu Christ. When man is in point of death, and hasteth fast to his end, then should no carnal friends, nor wife, nor children, nor riches, nor no temporal goods, be reduced [2] unto his mind, neither be communed of before him; only as much as spiritual health and profit of the sick man asketh and requireth.

In this matter that is of our last and most great need, all manner of points and sentences [3] thereof, and adverbs also that be put thereto, should most subtly and diligently be charged and considered of every man; [4] forasmuch as there shall no man be rewarded for his words alone, but for his deeds also joined and according to his words. As it is said in the book cleped COMPENDIUM OF THE TRUTH OF DIVINITY, the second book, the tenth chapter: That what man that lusteth, and will gladly die well and surely and meritorily, without peril, he must take heed visibly, and study and learn diligently this craft of dying, and the dispositions thereof abovesaid, while he is in heal; and not abide till the death entereth in him.

For sooth, dear sister or brother, I tell thee sooth, believe me thereof, that when death or great sickness

[1] *i.e.* suddenness. [2] *i.e.* brought back. [3] meanings.

[4] *Porro in materia ista . . . ponderentur singula puncta etiam sententie quibus adjecta sunt adverbia, eo quod non in verbis sed adverbis meremur* (*i.e.* it is not only what we do, but how we do it).

falleth upon thee, devotion passeth out from thee; and the more near they take thee and grip thee, the further fleeth devotion from thee. Sicker this is sooth, I know it by experience; for in sooth thou shalt have little devotion if thou be sore touched with sickness.[1] Therefore if thou wilt not be deceived or err—if thou wilt be sure—do busily what thou mayst while thou art in heal, and hast the use and freedom of thy five wits and reason well disposed, and while thou mayst be master of thyself and of thy deeds.

O Lord God how many, yea without number, (that) have abiden so to their last end have forslothed and deceived themselves everlastingly. Take heed, brother or sister, and beware, if ye list, lest it happen thee in the same wise. But let no man wonder, nor think that it is inconvenient that so great charge and diligence and wise disposition and providence, and busy exhortation should be had and ministered to them that be in point of death, and in their last end—as it is abovesaid—for they be in such peril and in so great need at that time, that, and it were possible, all a city should come together with all haste to a man that is nigh to the death or dying; as the manner is in some religious,[2] in which it is ordained that when a sick man is nigh the death, then every of the brothers shall, when they hear the table[3] smitten—what hour that ever it be, and where that ever they be—all things being left, hastily come

[1] Only in this MS. (Bod. 423).
[2] *i.e.* religious houses.
[3] A flat board which was struck instead of a bell.

to him that is a-dying. Therefore it is read that religious people and women—for the honesty of estate—should not run but to a man that is a-dying and for fire.[1]

CHAPTER VI

THE SIXTH CHAPTER CONTAINETH PRAYERS THAT SHOULD BE SAID UPON THEM THAT BE A-DYING OF SOME MAN THAT IS ABOUT THEM

LAST of all it is to be known that the prayers that follow may be conveniently said upon a sick man that laboureth to his end. And if it is a religious person, then when the covent is gathered together with smiting of the table, as the manner is, then shall be said first the litany, with the psalms and orisons that be used therewith. Afterward, if he live yet, let some man that is about him say the orisons that follow[2] hereafter, as the time and opportunity will suffer. And they may be often rehearsed again to excite the devotion of the sick man—if he have reason and understanding with him.

But nevertheless this ought not to be done of necessity, as though he might not be saved but if it were done; but for the profit and devotion of the sick that laboureth to his endward it may, and it is well done, that it be done so. But among seculars that be sick let these prayers be said; as the devotion and disposition, and the profit of them and others

[1] MS. fere = *ignem*. [2] MS. suen.

that be about them ask and require, and as the time will suffice.

But alas there be full few, not only among seculars but also in diverse religious that have the cunning of this craft, and will be nigh and assist to them that be in point of death and departing out of this world; asking them, and exhorting and informing and praying for them, as it is abovesaid—namely when they that be in dying would not, or hope not, to die yet, and so the sick men's souls stand in great peril.

In these prayers, if thou say them thyself, turn the words that should be turned, as thou shouldest do to say them thyself; for I write them as another should say them for thee.[1]

For that love that made Thee to be wounded and die for the heal and salvation of mankind, that were most worthy and most delicate,[2] Son [3] of God, of Thy blessed Father of Heaven, and for our sake made Man; sweet Lord Jesu, full of mercy, forgive Thy servant that he hath trespassed in thought, word, and deed, in all his affections, desires, motions, strengths, and wits of his soul and his body; and in very remission of them all forgive thy servant that he hath trespassed, give him that most sufficient amendment, by the which Thou washest away all the sins of the world, and in supplicion [4] of all his negligences, and put to him that holy con-

[1] Only in this MS. [2] *i.e.* lovely.
[3] 'loue,' probably a mis-writing for 'sone' since it = *filium*. [4] *i.e.* in supply of.

versation that Thou haddest from the hour of Thy conception, unto the hour of Thy death; and furthermore the fruit of all good deeds, the which have pleased Thee, and shall please Thee, in all Thy chosen people from the beginning of the world unto the end thereof. Sweet Lord Jesu, which livest and reignest with Thy Father and with the Holy Ghost, one very God withouten end. AMEN.

FOR THE UNION of the most fervent love that stirred and made Thee—life of all things that is living—to be incarnate of our Lady, and with great anguish of Thy spirit to die for charity and the love of us; we cry to the root of Thy most benign heart[1] that Thou forgive the soul of Thy servant all his sins; and with Thy most holy conversation and most worthy merit of Thy passion fulfil all his negligences and omissions, and make him to feel by experience the most superabundant greatness of Thy mercies, and us all; and specially this person, our brother, the which Thou hast disposed hastily[2] to be called before Thy glorious Majesty—in the most pleasant manner to Thee, and most profitable to him and us all. Make him to be presented to You with sweet patience, very repentance, and full remission; with rightful faith, stable hope, and perfect charity; that he may die blessedly, in perfect state, between Thy most sweetest clipping[3] and

[1] *ad medullam ben·gnissimi cordis tui.*
[2] *i.e.* hast made ready suddenly. [3] embracing.

most sweetest kissing, in to Thine everlasting worship and praising. AMEN.

ORATIO

INTO THE HANDS of Thine endless and unquenchable mercy, holy Father, rightful[1] and most beloved Father, we commend the spirit of our brother, Thy servant, after the greatness of love that the holy soul of Thy Blessed Son commended Himself to Thee on the cross; praying entirely[2] that for thilk inestimable charity that Thine Holy Godhead drew fully into Thyself that blessed soul of Thy Son, that now in his last hour Thou receive sweetly the spirit of our brother, Thy servant, in the same love. AMEN.

SAINT MICHAEL, THE ARCHANGEL of our Lord Jesu Christ, help us at[3] our high Judge. O thou most worthy giant and protector, that mayst never be overcome, be nigh to our brother, thy servant, labouring now sore in his end; and defend him mightily from the dragon of hell, and from all manner guile of wicked spirit. Furthermore we pray thee, that art so clear[4] and so worthy a minister of God, that in the last hour of the life of our brother thou wilt receive the soul of him easily and benignly into thine holy[5] bosom; and bring

[1] *i.e.* righteous. [2] sincerely. [3] with. [4] *praeclarum.*
[5] 'wholesome,' but the other MSS. have 'holy.'

her into (the) place of refreshing and of peace, and of rest. AMEN.

EVER CLEAN AND BLESSED MAIDEN MARY, singular help and succour in every anguish and necessity, help us sweetly, and show to our brother, thy servant, thy glorious visage now in his last end. And void[1] all his enemies from him, through the virtue of thy dear beloved Son, our Lord Jesu Christ, and of the holy Cross; and deliver him from all manner disease of body and soul, that he may thank and worship God withouten end. AMEN.

MY MOST SWEET REDEMPTOR, most merciful Jesu, and most benign Lord, for that sorrowful voice that Thou haddest in Thy manhood when Thou shouldest die for us, and were so consumed with sorrows and travails of Thy passion that Thou crydest[2] Thee forsaken of Thy Father; be not far from Thy brother, Your servant, but give him Thine help, of Thy mercy, in the hour of his death; and have mind of the grievous affliction and pain of his soul, the which in his last hour of passing, for failing of his spirits, hath no might to call upon Thee for help: but by the victory of the cross, and by virtue of Thine holy passion and Thine amorous death, think upon her thoughts of peace and not of affliction, but of mercy and comfort; and deliver her fully from all manner

[1] *i.e.* expel. [2] *i.e.* proclaimed by loud crying.

of anguishes. With the same hands that Thou didst suffer to be nailed on the cross for her sake with sharp nails, good Jesu and sweet Father, deliver her from the torments ordained for her, and bring her to everlasting bliss and rest, with a voice of exaltation and knowledging of Thy mercy. AMEN.

MOST MERCIFUL LORD JESU CHRIST, GOD'S SON, for the union of the recommendation that Thou commendest Thine holy soul to Thine heavenly Father, dying on the cross, we commend to Thine innumerable[1] pity the soul of our brother, Thy servant, praying Thy most merciful goodness that for all the worship and merit of Thy most holy soul, by the which all souls be saved and delivered from the debt of death, Thou have mercy upon the soul of our dear brother, Thy servant; delivering her mercifully from all miseries and pains, and for the love and mediation of Thy sweet Mother, bring her to contemplation of the joy of Thy most sweet and merciful sight everlastingly. AMEN.

MERCIFUL AND BENIGN GOD, That for the mickelness of Thy mercy doest away the sins of them that be verily repentant, and voidest the blames of sins that be passed and done before through grace of Thy forgiveness, we beseech that Thou look mercifully upon our brother,

[1] *i.e.* incapable of being reckoned or uttered = *ineffabilis*.

Thy servant, and graciously hear him asking, with all confession of his heart, remission of all his sins. Renew in him, most merciful Father, all thing that is corrupt in him by bodily frailty, or defouled with the fraud of the devil, and gather him to the unity of the body of Holy Church, and make him a member of Holy Redemption. Have mercy, Lord, upon his wailings, have mercy upon his tears, and admit to the sacrament of Thy reconciliation him that hath no trust but upon Thy mercy; by Our Lord Jesu Christ. Amen.

Dear Brother, I commend thee to Almighty God, and commit thee to Him, Whose creature thou art, that when thy manhood hath paid his debt by the mean of death, that thou turn again to God thy creature, That made thee of the slime of the earth. When thy soul passeth out of thy body, glorious companies of angels come against thee: the victorious host, worthy judges, and senators of the holy apostles meet with thee: the fair, white, shining company of holy confessors, with the victorious number of glorious martyrs, come about thee: the joyful company of holy virgins receive thee: and the worthy fellowship of holy patriarchs open to thee the place of rest and joy, and deem thee to be among them that they be among, everlastingly.

Know thou never that (which) is horrible in

darkness, that grinteth[1] in flaming fire. They that punish in torments give place to thee, and grieve thee not. They that follow Sathanas with all his servants, in the coming against thee, be a-ghast at the presence of holy angels, and flee into darkness of everlasting night; into the great tribulous sea of hell. Our lord ariseth and His enemies be dispartled[2] about; and flee, they that hate Him, from His visage. Fail they as the smoke faileth, and as the wax melteth against[3] the fire, so perish sinners from the face of God; and let rightful men eat and rejoice in the sight of God.[4] All the contrary legions and ministers of Sathanas be not hardy to let thy journey. Christ deliver thee from torment, that vouchsafed to die for thee. Christ, God's Son, bring thee to the merry joys of Paradise, and the very Shepherd know thee among His sheep. He assoil thee from all thy sins, and put thee on His right side; in the sort[5] of His chosen children, that thou may see thy Redemptor visage to visage, and presentially[6] assisting to Him, see with (thine) eyes the blessed everlasting truth openly; and among the blessed company of the children of God have thou, and rejoice in the joy of the contemplation of God without end. AMEN.

Ps. lxviii. 2.

[1] *i.e.* grindeth his teeth. [2] scattered.
[3] *i.e.* exposed to.
[4] *et justi epulentur et exultent in conspectum Dei.* [5] lot.
[6] *i.e.* as being present.

ORATIO

Go Christian Soul out of this world, in the Name of the Almighty Father that made thee of nought ; in the Name of Jesu Christ, His Son, that suffered His passion for thee ; and in the Name of the Holy Ghost, that was infounded[1] into thee. Holy angels, Thrones and Dominations, Princehoods, Protestates and Virtues, Cherubim and Seraphim, meet with thee. Patriarchs and prophets, apostles and evangelists, martyrs, confessors, monks and hermits, maidens and widows, children and innocents, help thee. The prayers of all priests and deacons, and all the degrees of Holy Church, help thee ; that in peace be thy place, and thy dwelling in heavenly Jerusalem everlastingly ; by the mediation of Our Lord Jesu Christ, that is Mediator between God and man. Amen.

EXPLICIT TRACTATUS UTILISSIMUS
DE ARTE MORIENDI

[1] shed.

NOTE ON THE BOOK OF THE CRAFT OF DYING

There are three manuscripts of this treatise in the Bodleian Library; the Douce MS. 322, the Rawlinson MS. C. 894, and the Bodleian MS. 423.[1] This transcription has been taken from the last of these, since it appears to be the earliest.[2] It is to be found in a large brown volume containing five different manuscripts bound together by Sir Thomas Bodley. Some are written on paper, and some on parchment. Our book is the fourth in order, written on parchment in a clear and careful hand, and dating probably from the middle of the fifteenth century. The headings to the chapters are in red, the capitals are in blue and red, and on the first page a border is outlined which has never been finished.

Like so many other English writings of this date *The Craft of Dying* has been ascribed to Richard Rolle. It may possibly have been translated by him into English, but the author of the older Latin original is unknown. It has been suggested that it was written by Jean le Charlier de Gerson, the famous Chancellor of Paris—known to us in connection with *De Imitatione Christi*, which some have attributed to him. Gerson certainly compiled a long treatise in Latin and French which he named the *Opusculum Tripartitum de Preceptis Decalogi, de Confessione, et de Arte Moriendi.*[3] But this book is very much shorter than the English version of *The Craft of Dying*, and there is nothing in it which corresponds to the first two chapters of the *Craft*; moreover, the

[1] I have collated these three MSS., and have drawn attention to differences of any interest in the footnotes.

[2] It is not mentioned by Dr Horstman. Besides the Douce and Rawl. MSS. his list contains: C.C.C. Oxfd. 220, Harl. 1706, Reg. 17 C. xviii., Addit. 10596, Ff. v. 45; *cf. The Library of English Writers*, vol. ii. p. 406.

[3] Published at Cologne *c.* 1470.

references in Chapters III. and V. of the Craft to "the noble" and "great clerk, the Chancellor of Paris,"[1] must be to Gerson.[2]

Indeed the whole question of the authorship and the various versions of the treatises which are in the catalogues generally included under the title *Ars Moriendi* is one of some difficulty and obscurity. There seem to be at the least three distinct books: the Latin treatise, of which this is a translation; the very popular block-books of the *Ars Moriendi*, of which many copies exist; and a rarer French book, *L'Art de bien Vivre et bien Mourire*, which seems to be related to the block-books.

The Latin treatise is found under three titles: *De Arte Moriendi; Tractatus de Arte Moriendi;* and *Speculum Artis Moriendi.* Many printed versions exist, the oldest of which is ascribed to Mathieu de Cracovie, Bishop of Worms, the date given being 1470 or 1472. Another edition was printed at Venice in 1478, and called: *Tractatus brevis ac valde utilis de arte et scientia bene moriendi.* It seems to be a compendium of the older version, and was attributed to Dom Caprianica, Cardinal de Fermo. Most of the later editions were printed at Paris, and contain additional prayers and admonitions, and in some cases verses, which are not found in any of the manuscripts nor in the earlier printed versions, and which I have not included here since they are of no special interest. When it has been necessary to refer to the Latin original I have had recourse to a beautiful manuscript in Magdalen College, Oxford, from which I have made an occasional quotation in a footnote.

I have not yet been able to trace the French versions from which Caxton tells us he has translated his tract "abridged of the art to learn well to die." *L'Art de bien Vivre et bien Mourire* is quite another book. It was published by Verard in Paris in 1493, and translated into very bad English in 1503, this translation being also issued by Verard. There are copies of both these in the Bodleian; and written on the cover of the English translation is a note stating that "This

[1] *cf.* pp. 24, 33.

[2] *cf.* my note on Caxton's Abridgment, p. 88.

was reproduced by Wynken de Worde, 'The craft to live and dye well,—made parfyte in our moder tongue; the 21st day of January 1505.'"

There is a copy of this reproduction of de Worde's in the John Rylands Library at Manchester, the only one as far as is known. Through the kind courtesy of the librarian there, who has sent me the transcription of a short passage, I have been able to compare them, and find that de Worde's reproduction is an improvement, both in spelling and English, upon the translation of 1505.

L'Art de bien Vivre et bien Mourire seems to have more in common with Gerson's *Opusculum Tripartitum*, for both contain discourses on the Lord's Prayer, the Ten Commandments, the Creed, the Sacraments, etc. Mr Bullen states that it also comprises "a complete translation into French of the letterpress of the block-book, accompanied by copies of all the wood engravings."[1]

The block-books of the *Ars Moriendi* are very numerous and interesting, and need really a volume to themselves. They seem to have been most popular in England, Germany and France, though we find copies in almost every European language. They generally contain eleven illustrations depicting the five great temptations which beset the soul at death. These temptations are embodied in the forms of hideous demons, which are repelled by angels and saints, and by Our Lady, who is the great interceder and last resource of the Dying Creature.

Our frontispiece is taken from the famous block-book in the British Museum, which was published at Cologne *c.* 1450. The artist probably belonged to the Lower Rhenish School. It represents the Good Angel coming to strengthen and console the dying man when tempted by the devil of Avarice. His Guardian Angel stands in front of him with his hand raised in exhortation, bearing a scroll with the words *Non sis avarus*. At the head of the bed stands Our Lady, beside her Blessed Son outstretched upon the cross.

[1] See his *Introduction to the "Ars Moriendi,"* pub. by the Holbein Society, 1851, p. 21.

On the other side of the crucifix is a figure which may represent the Good Shepherd, as close beside him there are three sheep, and he holds a staff in his hand. Behind this figure stand three women, and the head of a man is seen at the back. It is difficult to conjecture what they are meant to typify, unless those "other saints which the sick man may most have loved and honoured in his life," for they all look compassionately on him. Below is another angel, half hidden by a cloth which he holds in his hands, apparently trying to shield the figures of a man and woman from the sick man's gaze. On a scroll encircling his head are the words: "*Ne intende amicis.* Do not concern thyself with thy friends." Mr Bullen suggests that both may possibly be "disappointed expectants of sharing the dying man's wealth; or else the female figure representing his wife, and the male figure that of his physician."[1] But the words of the scroll lead us to suppose they symbolise the relations of the sick man, whom he has been exhorted to forget at the hour of his death, that he may give his mind more intently to the things which are not seen. In the other illustrations of the block-book hideous demons are depicted howling round the bed, or fleeing under it, but here (and partly this is the reason for its choice) only one impotent and angry devil is seen, ejaculating in despair *Quid faciam?*

In conclusion I can only say how sadly I am conscious of the inadequacy of these notes; but the longer one works among manuscripts and old reprints the more there seems left to be discovered, and my hope is that I may at least have cleared the ground so as to help another on the same quest.

---

[1] *Introduction to the "Ars Moriendi,"* p. 16.

THE ART AND CRAFT
TO KNOW WELL TO DIE

HERE BEGINNETH A LITTLE TREATISE SHORT AND ABRIDGED: SPEAKING OF THE ART AND CRAFT TO KNOW WELL TO DIE

WHEN it is so that what a man maketh or doeth, it is made to come to some end, and if the thing be good and well made, it must needs come to good end; then by better and greater reason every man ought to intend in such wise to live in this world, in keeping the commandments of God, that he may come to a good end; and that out of this world—full of wretchedness and tribulations—he may go to heaven, unto God and His saints, into joy perdurable.

But now in these days few there be that advise[1] them of their end so much as they ought to do, though they be sick, ancient or old; and to them cometh this folly by a foolish hope that every man, in what estate he be, hath an hope to live long. And therefore hath this present treatise been made; composed in short terms for to teach every man well to die whilst he hath understanding, health and reason, to the end that it is needful to him to be the better warned, informed and taught.

[1] *i.e.* consider, ponder on.

The which treatise is divided into six parts: of which the first treateth of the praising of death, and how one ought to die gladly.

The second treateth of the temptations that they have which be or lie in the article[1] of death.

The third treatise is of the questions that ought [to] be made to them then.

The fourth containeth a manner of instructions and of teaching that ought to be made to them.

The fifth of the remembrance that God hath won and suffered for us.

The sixth and last treateth of certain orisons and devout prayers that they ought to say if they may; or else ought to be said before them, by some that be assistant or present.

CHAPTER I

OF THE ALLOWING OR PRAISING OF THE DEATH: AND HOW ONE GLADLY OUGHT FOR TO DIE

As then the bodily death is the most fearful thing of all other things, so yet is the death of the soul of as much more terrible and reproachable,[2] as the soul is more noble and more precious than the body. And the death of sinners is right cursed and evil; but the death of just and true people is precious before God;

[1] *i.e.* the very moment.
[2] *i.e.* deserving of reproach, censurable.

for the dead men be well happy that die in our Lord.

To this purpose saith *Plato*: That continual remembrance of the death is sovereign wisdom. Also for truth the bodily death of good people alway is none other thing but the issue, or going out, of prison and of exile, and discharging of a right grievous burden, that is to wit of the body; finishing of all things, and end of all maladies and sicknesses, and also of all other strifes mortal. It is the voiding of this present wretchedness; it is consumption of all evils, and the breaking of all the bonds of this cursed and evil world; it is the payment of the debt of nature, return into the country, and entry into joy and glory. Therefore saith the wise man: That the day of the death is better than the day of the birth. But this word ought to be understood for them that be good only.

And therefore every good Christian man, and also every sinner verily contrite, ought not to be sorrowful nor trouble him of the temporal or bodily death, nor he ought not to fear nor doubt[1] it, for whatsomever matter or cause be laid to him, but he ought to suffer and receive it patiently and in thanks and gladly; in conforming himself plainly,[2] and in committing wholly his proper[3] will to God's will, like as (he) is bounden to him.

For well to die is gladly to die; and to con die is to have in all times his heart ready and apparelled to[4]

[1] dread. [2] *i.e.* yielding himself fully.
[3] *i.e.* own. [4] prepared for.

things heavenly and supernal. And that at every hour, when the death shall come to the person, that he be found ready; and that he receive it without any contradiction, but also joyfully, as he should abide the coming of his good friend. To this purpose saith the *Philosopher*: That natural reason well counselled judgeth that the good death ought better to be chosen than the evil life, and that one ought sooner to choose the bodily death than do anything against the weal of virtue.

Thus then it appeareth of the praising of the death; and that every good person and religious ought to desire departing of the body and soul for to be with our Lord Jesu Christ, and for to leave this present world for the better to live in the world to come.

CHAPTER II

THE TEMPTATIONS THAT THE PERSON HATH AT THE HOUR OF THE DEATH

It ought to be known and be believed certainly that they that be in the article of death have many grievous and strong temptations; verily such that in their life they never had like. And of these temptations there be five principal.

I. The First is of the Faith; for because that faith is foundation of all health, and that without faith it is impossible to please God. Therefore it is that then in this point the devil with all his might enforceth[1] him to trouble the person from his faith wholly, or at the least to make him to go out of the way from his faith; and laboureth then much strongly for to deceive him by some errors, superstitions, or heresy. And because every good Christian person is bound to believe, not only in the articles of the faith Catholic, but all the holy scripture; and ought to be subjugate and submit himself to all the statutes of the church of Rome, and firmly to abide and die in the same creance and belief. For else, if he should begin to err in any of the things abovesaid, then incontinent[2] he should go out of the faith of life and way of health.

Always [it] ought to be known certainly that in this temptation of the faith—or in other things following—the devil may not overcome the person as long as he shall have the usage of his free will well disposed, if by his own agreement he will not consent to the devil. And therefore it is good, and a thing much profitable, that about them that travail in the article of death be repeated with an high voice the Credo and symbol of the faith, to the end that by that means the person dying be the more hearted and encouraged in the constancy of the faith. To the end also that the devils, which have horror to hear it, be put aback and driven away. [So] certainly [was] the faith of the true ancient men, as sometime were Abraham, Isaac and Jacob; also of some paynims and gentiles as were Job, Raab, Ruth, Achior, and other semblable. And also they of the

[1] striveth. [2] straightway.

apostles and of the innumerable martyrs, confessors and virgins. The faith of such people ought much to comfort[1] the sick man to the constancy and steadfastness of the faith. For by faith all they of time past, and of this present time, have pleased God ; and it is impossible to please God without faith. For faith may all, and very faith getteth all that it requireth.

II. The Second Temptation is against Hope, by Despair. For a person ought to have all hope and confidence in God. And it happeth then, when a person being sick in his body is tormented with great pain and sorrows, that the devil enforceth to bring to him sorrow upon sorrow, in bringing before his remembrance all his sins, by all the ways that he may—at least them that he never confessed him of—to the end that by that means he draw him into desperation. Upon this purpose saith *Innocent* : That every Christian person—be he good or evil—before that his soul issueth out of his body seeth our Lord Jesu Christ set in the cross. That is to wit : the evil to their confusion, to the end that they have shame and displeasure that they have not gotten in their life the fruit of the Redemption ; and the good to their honour and pleasure.

Natheless none ought to have despair in no wise, how much felon and evil he hath been. Though that he had commised as many murders and thefts as there be drops of water and small gravel in the sea, yet were it so that of them he had never done

[1] *i.e.* strengthen.

penance nor confessed them, as long as the patience of our Lord holdeth him in this mortal life, and that he have power and might to repent him ;—notwithstanding that then by force of malady and sickness he may not confess him. For contrition only, within forth, may suffice in such a case. For God despiseth never a contrite heart and humble ; and also the pity and mercy of God is much more than any iniquity or wickedness.

And therefore the sin and crime of desperation is to him that only by which he may not be saved nor guarished ;[1] for by this sin God, which is right piteous, is overmuch offended, and the other sins be so much more aggrieved ;[2] and also the pain eternal is by so much more augmented into the infinite. The evils and sins commised and passed grieve not so much but despair displeaseth more. And therefore none ought to despair of the mercy of God, though that he only had commised all the sins of the world ; though yet he suppose [himself] to be of the number of [those] that be damned.

In truth the disposition of the body of our Lord Jesu Christ hanging on the cross ought much to induce a sick person, paining to the death, to have very hope and confidence in God. For He hath the head inclined and bowed to kiss us ; the arms stretched abroad for to embrace us ; the hands pierced and opened for to give us ; the side open for to love us ; and all His body stretched for to give Himself all to us. Hope

[1] *i.e.* that one sin of which he cannot be saved or cured.
[2] aggravated.

then is a virtue much lowable[1] and of great merit before God.

To this purpose come many examples: as of Saint Peter, which renyed and forsook Jesu Christ; of Saint Paul which persecuted Holy Church; of Saint Matthew and of Zacchæus, which were publicans; of Mary Magdalene the sinner; of the woman that was taken in adultery; of the thief that hanged on the right side of Jesu Christ; of Saint Mary Egyptian. And of many more other, which were great sinners and horrible, which alway set all their hope in God and were saved.

III. The Third Temptation that the devil maketh to them that die is by Impatience; that is against Charity. For by charity we be holden to love God above all things. Now is it thus that to them that die cometh right great sorrow and pain of heart and of body, be it that the death come naturally, or that it come by any other evil accident. For by pain and sorrow many there be that [have] been impatient and grutching, and die in such wise as they seem mad, or out of their wit, as it appeareth oft. Wherefore it is certain that such people be out of very love and charity, and that they love not God sufficiently. And therefore it is necessary to every man that will die, that in what sickness be it, short or long, that he murmur nor grutch not, but suffer it patiently. For we suffer by good right all the evils that come to us, and yet be not the passions of this world condign nor worthy to the glory to come. This is then a thing

[1] *i.e.* to be praised.

much unjust if of the just passions we murmur or grutch; for like as the soul is possessed in patience, and by murmurs the soul is lost and damned. Ought not then our Lord thus [to] enter into His glory: and know ye that the infirmity before the death is like as a purgatory, so that it be suffered like as it appertaineth, that is to say patiently, gladly, and agreeably. And it cometh by divine dispensation that to the longest vice and sin is given the longest malady; and that God mercifully sendeth temporal tarrying, to the end that he go not to eternal pain.

It appeareth then that all maladies and sicknesses of the body, whatsoever they be, ought by reason to be suffered without grutching; for he that well loveth, to him is nothing impossible.

IV. The Fourth Temptation of them that die is the Complacence or pleasing of himself; and that is a spiritual pride by the which the devil assaileth most them that be devout. And it happeth when the devil hath not mowe,[1] nor can not induce the man to go out of the faith, nor to make him fall into desperation or into impatience, that then he assaulted him by complacence, or pleasing of himself; to him presenting in his heart such things: O how thou art firm and steadfast in the faith! O how thou art sure in hope! O how thou art strong and patient! O how thou hast done many good deeds! or such things semblable, for to put him in vainglory. But against this let none give to himself no manner praising, nor avaunt him; nor none glorify himself of his

[1] *i.e.* hath not power, or might.

good deeds, nor presume nothing of himself, nor not attribute himself to do nothing well; for this complacence is vainglory, and it may be so great that by it a man might be damned.

A man nigh his death ought to be well advised when by such pride he feels himself tempted, that then he humble and meek himself so much the more; that he withdraw him in thinking [on] his wretchedness and his sins. For none is certain if he be digne or worthy to have deserved the love of God, or the hate of God. Natheless none ought to despair; but right always to address his heart to God by good hope, in thinking and considering the mercy of God to be above all his works.

V. The Fifth Temptation that most troubleth the secular and worldly men is the over great occupation of outward things and temporal: as toward his wife, his children and his friends carnal; toward his riches or toward other things which he hath most loved in his life. And therefore whomsoever will well and surely die, he ought to set simply and all from him all outward things and temporal, and ought all to commit to God fully. And if he so do, in suffering patiently the pain of death he satisfieth for all his venial sins; and, what more is, he bringeth something for to satisfy for the deadly sins. But it happeth not oft that any be found—be he secular or regular—that hopeth not but to escape from death; and always this foolish hope is a thing right perilous and much disordered[1] in every Christian man, and

[1] *i.e.* disorderly or unruly.

that oft cometh by instinction[1] of the devil; the which may not surmount the man in none of the said temptations, nor in none other whatsomever they be, but if[2] the man, having the usage of reason, will by his own agreement consent to him. For our enemy is so feeble that he may not overcome but him that will be vanquished; and God is so good and just that He shall not suffer us to be tempted above that which we may not withstand; but He shall do to us aid and profit with the temptation, to the end that we may sustain it.

And every man ought to know that the victory of temptations cometh alway by humility and meekness; for they that have not in them the wind of pride fall never into the furnace. And therefore every sinner ought wholly to meek himself under the mighty hand of God, to the end that by the help of our Lord he may obtain victory in all temptations, in all sicknesses, and in all tribulations of pain and of sorrow, unto the death inclusively.

CHAPTER III

OF THE DEMANDS AND QUESTIONS THAT OUGHT TO BE MADE TO THE SICK PERSON

THEN ought to be made askings and demands of them that be in the article of death, as long as they have the usage of reason and of speech; to the end that if

[1] instigation. [2] except.

they be less or worse disposed than it appertaineth ;[1] and that they be by that moyen[2] the better informed and comforted. After [the saying of] *Saint Anselm* these manners of demands ought to be said thus, as here followeth :

> Thou, brother or sister, (in naming the name) art thou joyful that thou diest in the faith of our Lord Jesu Christ ? And he or she ought to answer yea.
>
> Repentest thee of that (or such thing) whereto thou wert inclined ? Answer : Yea.
>
> Hast thou will to amend thee if thou haddest space to live ? Answer : Yea.
>
> Believest thou that thou mayst not be saved but by the death of our Lord Jesu Christ and by His passion ? Answer : Yea.

Yield to Him thankings with all thine heart whiles that thy soul is in thee, and constitute and set all thy trust in His death that thou abidest now presently,[3] and have no trust in any other thing. Give thyself over, cover thee all and wrap thee in this death ; and if God will judge thee, say thus to Him :

Lord, I put Thy death between Thy judgment and me ; other wise I will not debate nor strive against Thee. I offer Thee the merits of Thy right worthy passion, by the merit that I ought to have gotten—which I have nothing done, and woe is me

[1] *i.e.* is befitting or proper. [2] means.
[3] *i.e.* without delay, immediately.

therefore now ; and [I] recommend at this time my spirit into Thy hands.

These demands and questions beforesaid ought to be said, as well to religious as to seculars, to the end that in the pain of death they be the better informed of their estate. And if the time suffer it, men ought yet to say this that followeth :

> Believest thou all the principal articles of the faith of Holy Church, and all the Holy Scripture in all things ; and the exposition of the catholic and all holy doctors, of our Mother, Holy Church ? Answer : Yea.
>
> Despisest thou and reprovest all heresies, errors and superstitions, which be reproved of Holy Church ? He ought to answer : Yea.
>
> Knowledgest thou that oft, and in many manners, thou hast right grievously offended thy Maker ? Answer : Yea.

As saith *Saint Bernard* there is none saved without (to have) knowledge of himself; for of this knowledge groweth humility which is mother of health.

Yet ought to be demanded :

> Brother or sister, sorrowest thou for all thy sins which thou hast commised against the majesty, the love, the goodness of God ; and of the good deeds that thou hast not done ; and of the graces of God of which thou hast been negligent ? He ought to answer : Yea.
>
> Thou oughtest not only to sorrow for doubt of the death which thou attendest, or for any

pain, but for the love of God or of justice; and thou requirest pardon with all thy heart. Answer: Yea.

Desirest thou also that thy heart may be meeked to the knowledge of the defaults of which thou art not remembered presently,[1] to the end that thou mayst duly repent them? He ought to answer: Yea.

Purposest thou veritably to amend thee, if thou mightest live and be whole, and that thou wouldest never sin deadly in earnest; and haddest liever to lose the best thing that thou lovest—yea the bodily life—before thou wouldest offend thy Maker; and to pray God with good heart that He will give thee grace for to continue in this purpose? Answer: Yea.

Forgivest and pardonest thou with good heart, for the love of God, all that have been trespassed to thee in word or in deed? He ought to answer: Yea.

Requirest[2] thou also for the love of God, of whom thou hopest to receive forgiveness, that that thou hast trespassed ever to any other, [of] that thou mayst be quit and forgiven? Answer: Yea.

Wilt thou the things that thou hast taken and holden unduly be by thee restored wholly, like as thou art bounden, and after the value of thy faculty,[3] unto the renunciation of all thy

[1] now. [2] requestest or desirest.
[3] resources or possessions.

goods, if otherwise thou mightest not make satisfaction? He ought to answer: Yea.

Believest thou that our Lord Jesu Christ be dead for thee; and that otherwise thou mightest not be saved, but by the merit of His precious passion; and thankest Him therefore with all thy heart? Answer: Yea.

In truth whosomever shall mowe[1] affirmatively to answer these askings beforesaid, with good conscience and very faith without feigning, he shall have evident sign and argument of health; and (that) he shall be of the number of them that thall be saved, if he die in this point.[2]

And if there be none to demand him he ought to return to himself and to demand himself, in considering the most subtly that he shall con mowe[3] if he be disposed like as is said; for without this disposition may no man by any manner be saved. And whomsoever shall feel himself thus well disposed, he ought to commend him all to the passion of our Lord Jesu Christ; and to put himself all in remembrance and in meditation of the same, as he shall mowe, and that as his infirmity shall suffer him. And by this moyen be surmounted and overcome all the temptations of the devil, and his right subtle awaits and fallacies.[4]

[1] *i.e.* be able.
[2] this moment of time.
[3] be able to have power to.
[4] *i.e.* snares and delusions.

CHAPTER IV

[AN INSTRUCTION WITH CERTAIN OBSECRATIONS TO THEM THAT SHALL DIE]

Saint Gregory saith that all the action and work of our Lord Jesu Christ ought to be our instruction, and therefore every good Christian person disposed well to die ought to do, after his manner and possibility, in his last end like as did our Lord when He died on the cross.

Now it is so that our Lord did five things principally hanging on the cross. He adored and prayed, He wept, He cried, He commended His soul to God, and He yielded to Him His spirit. Thus semblably every sick man, constituted in the article of[1] death, ought to adore and pray;—at least in his heart, if he may not speak. For as saith *Saint Isidore*: It availeth more to pray with heart, in silence and without speaking, than by words only without taking heed of the thought.

Secondly he ought to weep, not with his bodily eyes only, but with the tears of his heart, in repenting verily himself.

Thirdly he ought strongly to cry from the depths of his heart, and not by voice. For God beholdeth more the desire of the heart than the sound of the voice. Also to cry with the heart is none other thing,

[1] placed at the point of.

but strongly to desire remission of his sins and to come to everlasting life.

Fourthly he ought to commend his soul to God, saying: IN MANUS TUAS, etc.

Fifthly he ought to yield his spirit to God voluntarily, in conforming him all to the will of God like as it appertaineth, and in saying, if he may, the obsecrations that follow:

TO THE TRINITY

SOVEREIGN DEITY, right great Bounty, excellent and glorious Trinity, Sovereign Dilection,[1] Love, and Charity, have mercy on me, sinner, for I commend to Thee my spirit, my God, Father right piteous. Father of mercy give Thy mercy to this poor creature. Help me now in my last necessity. Lord, succour my poor soul, helpless now and desolate, to the end that it be not devoured by the hounds infernal. My right sweet and best beloved, Lord Jesu Christ, Son of the living God, for the love and honour, and by the virtue of Thy precious passion, command Thou, I Thee pray, that I be now received among the number of Thy chosen blessed souls. My Saviour and my Redeemer, I yield me all to Thee; refuse me not. I come to Thee; put me not from Thee.

LORD JESU CHRIST, I ask of Thee heaven; nothing for the love of my merits, for I am

[1] *i.e.* spiritual love.

nothing but dust and ashes, and a sinner right miserable; but I demand of Thee, in the virtue and in the value of Thy right holy passion, by the which Thou hast willed to redeem me which am a right miserable sinner with Thy much precious blood. Lord Jesu Christ, Son of the living God, I Thee supplicate meekly, by that bitterness of death which for me Thou sufferedst in the tree of the cross, and in especial at that hour when Thy right holy soul issued out of Thy precious holy body, that Thou have mercy on my most wretched soul at his departing.

Also, if he may, he ought to say three times the
Ps. cxv. 16. verse that followeth. DIRUPISTI DOMINE VINCULA MEA, TIBI SACRIFICABO HOSTIAM LAUDIS, ET NOMEN DOMINI INVOCABO. That is to say: Lord Thou hast broken my bonds; I shall sacrifice to Thee an host of praising, and shall call on the name of the Lord. For *Saint Isidore* saith that this verse is believed to be of so much virtue that if a man by very confession saith [it] in the end of his life, his sins be to him forgiven.

After these things the sick man ought, if he may, much entirely, with heart and mouth, the best wise that he shall mowe, require and call unto his help the right glorious Virgin Mary, which is the very mean[1] of all sinners, and she that addresseth[2] them in their necessity; saying to her in this manner:

QUEEN OF HEAVEN, Mother of mercy, and Refuge of sinners, I meekly beseech thee that

[1] mediator. [2] *i.e.* redresseth.

thou wilt reconcile me to thy dear Son, in calling His worthy goodness for me, unworthy sinner, that for the love of thee He will pardon and forgive me my sins, and bring me into His glory.

He ought afterward, if he may, call on the holy Angels, in saying:

Ye Spirits of Heaven, Angels much glorious, I beseech you that ye will be assistant[1] with me that now beginneth to depart, and that ye deliver me mightily from the awaits and fallacies of mine adversaries; and that it please you to receive my soul into your company. The principal, my leader and my good angel, which by our Lord art deputed to be my warden and keeper, I pray and require thee that thou now aid and help me.

And after he ought to require the apostles, the martyrs, the confessors and the virgins, and in especial all the saints that he most loved ever.

After all these things he ought to say three times, if he may, these words that follow; which is said to be made and composed by *Saint Austin*:

The Peace of our Lord Jesu Christ; the virtue of His holy passion; the sign of the holy cross; the entireness of the humility of the Virgin Mary; the blessing of all the saints; the keeping of the angels; and the suffrages of all the chosen of God; be between me and all

[1] *i.e.* present.

mine enemies, visible and invisible, in the hour of my death. AMEN.

And if the sick man or woman may, nor can not, say the orisons and prayers beforesaid, some of the assistants[1] ought to say them before him with a loud voice, in changing the words there as they ought to be changed. And the sick person, as far as he hath the usage of reason, ought to hearken and pray with his heart, and desire as much as he shall mowe; and so praying, render and yield his soul to God and without fail he shall be saved.

CHAPTER V

[AN INSTRUCTION UNTO THEM THAT SHALL DIE]

YET ought it to be known that every person having the love and dread of God in himself, and also the cure of souls, ought much busily and diligently induce and admonish the sick person constituted in peril of body or of soul, that first, hastily and principally, he purvey for him, without any delay, for remedy of medicine ghostly and spiritual. For it happeth oft that the infirmity and sickness of the body taketh his beginning of[2] the languor of the soul. And therefore the pope commanded straitly to all leeches and physicians of the body that to no manner sickness they minister nor give bodily medicine till that they have admonished and warned them to get and take

[1] *i.e.* bystanders.

[2] *i.e.* from.

first the spiritual medicine ; that is, to wit, in receiving devoutly the sacraments of Holy Church, in ordaining his testament, and in disposing lawfully his house and other goods and needs. And there ought not to be given to any sick person over much hope of recovering his bodily health. Howbeit oft times many do the contrary, in prejudice of their souls, yea, to them otherwhile[1] that draw to their death. And it happeth oft that they will not hear of death, and so by such false comfort, and by such faint trust of health, the sick person falleth into damnation. And therefore the sick person ought to be exhorted and desired that by very contrition and by very confession he procure the health of his soul.

Also that same may much avail for the health of the body, if it be to him expedient, and he shall be better appeased and more assured. For it seldom happeth, saith *Saint Gregory*, that very contrition be in the end, and that the penance that the sick men or women have then be very and sufficient to their health ; and they in especial,—as it is known in all the time of their life they never kept the commandments of God, or their vows voluntarily, but only faintly and by semblance.

Yet ought every man to induce him that is in the article of death that, after the possibility, and by reason of thought, he do pain and labour to have very and ordered patience ; that is to say, that, notwithstanding [the] sorrow and dread which then languish, he use reason as much as he shall

[1] at times.

mowe; and that he enforce him to have voluntary displeasure for his sins for the love of God; and that he resist his evil inclination used, in which he hath before taken delectation; and that he do pain to have displaisance as much as he shall mowe, howbeit that it be short. But to the end that he run not into despair [there] ought to be proposed to him and laid before [him] the things that were said in the second part of this present treatise upon the temptation of desperation. He ought also to be admonished to be couraged and strong against all other temptations there declared. Also be he admonished to die as a very and true Christian man (or woman); and that he take heed that he be not bound in the bond of excommunication; and that with all his might he submit him to the ordinance of our Mother, Holy Church, to the end that he be saved.

Item[1] if the sick man have long space of time, and that he be not oppressed of hasty death,[2] the assistants ought to read before him histories and devout orisons, which before he delighted and took pleasure in; and men ought to remember him of God's commandments, to the end that he think the more profoundly if he could find anything in himself that he hath against the said commandments commised and trespassed. And if he be so sick that he hath lost the usage of speech, and hath his knowledge whole and entire, he ought to answer to these things by some sign outward, or by whole consenting of heart, for that sufficeth to his salvation.

[1] Also. [2] *i.e.* surprised by sudden death.

Alway ought [it] to be taken heed that the interrogations be made before or that the sick man lose the usage of speech; and if the answers of the sick person appear not sound nor sufficient to his salvation, let there be put thereto remedy—by necessary information—by the best manner that may be.

And also [it] ought to be showed to the sick person the great peril that might fall and come to him, notwithstanding though he thereby should be afeared. For better it is that by fear and wholesome dread he have compunction and be saved, than by blandishing dissolution,[1] or by noyous comfort, he be damned. In truth this thing is much strange and over perilous, and contrary to the faith and Christian religion, but it is a thing diabolical, that to a Christian man, being in the article of death, for to hide from him the peril of the death of his soul, and that by human dread men dare not trouble him.

Contrary to this did *Isaye* the prophet when he feared[2] wholesomely the King Ezechias, lying sick unto the death, saying to him that he should die of that sickness; and nevertheless yet he died not. In like wise did *Saint Gregory*, when he feard wholesomely his monk—which was constituted in the article of death—for his propriety.[3]

Item [there] ought to be presented to the sick person the image of the crucifix, which alway should be among the sick people, and also the image of our Blessed Lady, and of other saints which the sick man

[1] softening. [2] *i.e.* made to fear.
[3] appropriation of goods.

hath most loved and honoured in his life. Also (there) ought to be about them holy water, and oft cast upon them and about them to the end that the devils be put a-back from them. And if because of shortness of time all these things aforesaid may not be done, yet they ought at least to purpose to them[1] the orisons and prayers which [are] addressed unto our Lord Jesu Christ. And there ought never to be brought to their remembrance the carnal friends, nor wife, nor children, nor riches, nor other goods temporal, but only as much as the spiritual health of the sick person demanded and requireth.

Whosomever then will learn to die let him come and learn all the things foresaid before, or he have need in the article of necessity. For in truth in grievous infirmity the devotion of the person goeth away and passeth ; and as much more as the sickness approacheth or increaseth, so much more the devotion fleeth from him. If thou wilt not then err nor be deceived, and that thou wilt be sure, do instantly all that thou mayst good, whiles that thou art whole and sound, and that thou hast the usage of reason and [art] well disposed, and that thou mayst be lord of all thy feats.[2]

O how much people, truly without number, have deceived themselves and bound themselves in abiding the last necessity ! And always it ought not to seem to none incongruous nor marvellous, (but) that it ought to [be] shown to them that die by some

[1] *i.e.* present to their mind.
[2] 'faytte' = actions, conduct.

diligent cure, by busy disposition and also by studious exhortation ; for without doubt such force and necessity runneth upon them suddenly, that if it were possible all a whole city ought [to] run hastily to a person that dieth.

CHAPTER VI

THE ORISONS AND PRAYERS THAT OUGHT TO BE SAID UPON THE SICK PERSON IN THE ARTICLE OF DEATH

FINALLY it ought to be known that the orisons which follow ought to be said upon, or over, a sick person, above the prayers that our Mother, Holy Church, hath accustomed to say over the sick persons labouring to the death.

And if the sick person be [a] religious the covent ought to be assembled by the table[1] as it is accustomed ; and after they ought to say the litany with the orisons, and the psalms ordinary and accustomed. After the which may be said the prayers that follow, as long as the time shall suffice ; and [they] may be rehearsed again divers times for to move the sick person the more to devotion, if he hath yet the usage of reason. And this is not done for necessity, but for the profit and devotion of the sick person.

And as touching the sick persons, seculars [there]

[1] A flat board which was struck in place of a bell.

ought to be said the orisons that follow; after that the disposition and devotion of the sick person, and the commodity[1] of the time, and if the assistants requireth. But few people or none be at this day that have the knowledge of this art.

Lord Jesu Christ, son of the fatherly charity, I beseech Thee by the Love that Thou, right much worthy, right innocent and most delicate, madest Thyself to be as man, to be wounded and die for the health of man, that Thou wilt pardon and forgive this Thy servant N. Jesus right merciful, forgive him all that by thought, by word or by deed, by affections or movings,[2] by his strength and by his wit, of body and of soul, he hath trespassed. And for remission, give to him, Lord, that right sufficient emendation by the which Thou unboundest the sins of all the world; and, for the fulfilling of all negligences, join to him that right ready and valiant conversation[3] that Thou haddest, sith and from the hour of Thy conception unto the hour of Thy death.

And moreover give to him the fruit of all the good works made and done by all the chosen saints, sith the beginning of the world unto the end. *Qui vivis et regnas Deus per omnia secula seculorum.*

In the honour of the right fervent love by

[1] convenience or supply of.
[2] either 'emotions' or 'motives.'
[3] *i.e.* behaviour or manner of life.

the which the Life of all living constrained Thee to be incarnate, and in anguish of spirit [1] to die on the cross, we remember on,[2] anew, (of) Thy right benign heart to the end that to this Thy servant, N. our brother, Thou put away all his sins, and that Thou forgive him all, by Thy right holy conversation and by the merit of Thy right holy passion ; that Thou make him to experiment the superabundant multitude of Thy miserations ;[3] and that Thou make ready us all, and in especial this person our brother, N., whom Thou hast disposed hastily to call to Thee by right pleasant manner ; and that it be to him right profitable by Thy sweet patience, by very penance, by plain [4] remission, by rightful faith, by steadfast hope, and by right perfect charity ; in such wise that in right perfect state he may blessedly depart and expire between Thy right sweet embracements and company, to Thy praising eternal. AMEN.

TO GOD THE FATHER

INTO THE HANDS of Thy mercy inestimable, holy Father, just Father, and much beloved, we commend the soul of Thy servant, N. our brother. In praising Thee humbly after the greatness of the love by the which the right holy soul of Thy Son commended Him to Thee

[1] 'anguyasshous esperyte.' [2] remind, or recall to.
[3] i.e. compassion. [4] complete.

on the cross; that by the inestimable charity of dilection,[1] by the which Thou, which art Divine Paternity, drewest to Thee the same right holy soul, Thou wilt at this last hour of (the) death of this Thy servant, N. our brother, receive in the same love his spirit. AMEN.

To God the Son

O MY MUCH LOVED REDEEMER, right piteous,[2] Jesus right benign, we pray Thy lacrimable[3] voice, by the which in Thy humanity, when Thou shouldest for us die, Thou wert consumed by labours and sorrows, in such wise that Thou wert left of Thy Father, that Thou withdraw not the help and aid of Thy mercy from this N. Thy servant, our brother, unto this hour and moment of his affliction; and the consumption of his spirit suffer not in this extreme hour of his death: but by the triumph of Thine holy cross, and by virtue of Thine healthful passion, and of Thy bitter death, think on him. Think of peace and not of affliction, and deliver his soul from all anguishes; and with the same hands the which, for love of him, Thou didst suffer to be fixed and nailed to the cross with right sharp nails, good Jesus, much sweet Father and Lord, deliver his soul from the torments which be deputed to him,

[1] *i.e.* spiritual love,—of God.
[2] *i.e.* pitiful.
[3] *i.e.* voice of lamentation.

and bring him to eternal rest with voice of exultation and of confession. AMEN.

O SWEET JESU, SON OF THE LIVING GOD, right merciful Lord, in union with that commendation by the which, in dying on the cross, Thou commendest Thy right holy soul to Thy heavenly Father, we commend to Thine ineffable pity the soul of this Thy servant, N., our brother; (in) requiring and praying Thy right merciful bounty that by the merit and honour of Thy much holy soul, by the which all souls be saved and from (the) death duly delivered, that it may please Thee, merciful Lord, to deliver this soul from all pains and miseries; and that for the love and intercession of Thy right sweet Mother, thou wilt conduct and lead it to behold the glory of this glorious vision. AMEN.

GOD RIGHT MIGHTY, debonair and merciful, which that, after the multitude of Thy mercy, effacest and puttest away the sins of them that be repentant, and that by pardon and remission voidest the culpe and blame of all sins; behold with pity (upon) this Thy servant, N., our brother, which with all confession of heart requireth of Thee pardon and remission of all his sins. Accord and grant it to him, we pray Thee, and renew in him, much piteous Father, all that which by worldly frailty hath been in him corrupt, and all that which by fraud diabolic hath been in him violated and despoiled, and assemble him in the unity of our Mother, Holy Church, as one of the number of Redemption. Lord have mercy on his wailings, have mercy on his tears, and bring him to the sacrament of Thine holy reconciliation; for he hath no trust but in Thine infinite mercy.

To Our Blessed Lady

O right entire, and eternal blessed Virgin, glorious Maid, aideress and helper of all anguish and necessity, succour us sweetly now; and show to thy servant here, N., our brother, thy gracious visage in this last necessity. Withdraw and put from him all his enemies, by the virtue of thy right dear Son, our Lord Jesu Christ, and by His holy cross and passion; and deliver him from all anguish of body and soul, to the end that to God our Lord he yield praising without end. Amen.

To Saint Michael

Saint Michael Archangel of God, succour us now before the right high Judge. O champion invincible, be thou present now and assist to this, N., our brother, which strongly laboureth towards his end, and defend him mightily from the dragon infernal, and from all the frauds of the evil spirits. O yet furthermore, we pray thee, which art the right clear and much fair shower of the divinity, to the end that in this last hour of the life of this N. our brother, thou wilt benignly and sweetly receive his soul into thy right holy bosom ; and that thou wilt bring him in the place of refreshing, of peace and rest. AMEN.

TO THE SICK PERSON AT HIS END

Right dear brother, or sister, I commend thee to God Almighty, and commit thee to Him of whom thou art creature, to the end when, by thy death, thou shalt have paid the duty of human nature, thou mayst return to thy Maker, which of the slime of the earth formed thee, [and] thy soul issue and go out of thy body when it shall please God.

The right splendant company of angels be at thy departing and meet thee ; the right clear sénate of apostles will diffend thee ; the victories of martyrs may meet thee ; the company adorned with shining confessors will environ thee ; the assembly of the right joyous virgins take and receive thee ; and the bosom of the blessed rest of patriarchs will open to thee, and join them with thee, and make thee to deserve to be among the assistants with thee : that thou avoid all that in darkness is horrible, all that in flames burneth and straineth, and all that which travaileth in torments. So depart from thee right black Sathanas, with all his cruel satellites, and the good angels of God may accompany thee in thy coming to glory. Flee from thee that felon Sathanas, and flee he into that stinking prison of darkness eternal.

So grant, God, that his enemies be dissipated, and they that hate him flee before his face. Defail they like as smoke faileth, and as the sinners perish before the face of God ; and the just persons come and enjoy them in the sight of God, and delight them in gladness. All the legions of hell and the ministers of satan be confounded in the fire, and be they ashamed and confounded ; nor have they none hardiness to let nor hinder [1] thy way. Jesu Christ deliver thee from torment, which for thee deigned to die on the cross, and constitute thee among the sweet and flowering places of paradise. The same very Pastor and Herdman know thee among His sheep ; which forgive to thee all thy sins, and set thee on His right side and in the party of His chosen people, and that thou may see face to face thy Creator and Maker. And that being with Him present and assistant, thou mayst behold His right manifest verity, and constituted without end among the companies well blessed, thou mayst joy in divine contemplations, world without end. AMEN.

CHRISTIAN SOUL, depart thee from this world when it shall please God, in the Name of the

[1] 'empeshe.'

Father, which thee created; in the Name of Jesu Christ, His son, which for thee suffered death; and in the Name of the Holy Ghost, which hath shed in thee His grace. Come to thy meeting and succour thee the holy Angels of God, the Archangels, the Virtues, the Potestates, the Dominations, the Thrones, the Cherubins, the Seraphins. Come to thine help and aid the patriarchs and prophets, the apostles and evangelists, the matrons and confessors, the monks and hermits, the virgins and widows, the children and innocents. Also help thee the prayers and visions of all priests and deacons, and of them of all degrees of the Church Catholic; to the end that thy place be in peace, and that thine habitation be in celestial Jerusalem. *Per Christum Dominum nostrum.* AMEN.

Like as the health of every man consisteth in the end, [let] every man then much busily take heed to purvey him for to come to a good end, whiles that he hath time and leisure. To this might much well serve a fellow and true friend, devout and comendable, which in his last end [may] assist him truly; and that he comfort and courage him in steadfastness of the faith, with good patience and devotion, with good confidence and perseverance. And that over him [they] say all these said orisons, well entently and devoutly, whiles that he is in travail of death. But always, for to come to the effect of these prayers, is all necessary the disposition of him that dieth, like as it hath been said heretofore. And therefore to every person that well and surely will die [it] is of necessity that he learn to die, or the death come and prevent him.

Thus endeth the tract abridged of the art to learn well to die: translated out of the French into English, by William Caxton. The xv. day of June, the year of our Lord a M iiij C lxxxx.

NOTE ON CAXTON'S ABRIDGMENT

NOT many copies of this book exist. There is a perfect copy in the British Museum[1]—of which this is a transcription, another belonging to Lord Spencer of Althorp, besides one in the National Library at Paris, and a copy in the Bodleian from which the last page is missing.

Judging from the colophon Caxton has evidently had some French translation of the *Speculum Artis Moriendi* before him; which he has abridged, all save the prayers. The date given is 1490, that is to say the year before his death, and it is of interest to find that a year later, the actual year of his death, he is making a still further abridgment of this same treatise.[2] There is no title page, and his No. 6 type is the only one used.

It is worth noting that in the complete version of *The Craft of Dying* there is no exhortation which quite corresponds to the one which Caxton places at the end of this abridgment, and at the beginning of his shorter tract. It occurs, however, both in the block-book, and in Gerson. In the block-book it is found, as here, at the end, and runs thus: "Sed heu, pauci sunt qui in morte proximis suis fideliter assistunt, interrogando, monendo, et pro ipsis orando; præsertim cum ipsi morientes nondum mori velin, et animæ morientum sæpe miserabiliter periclitantur."

Gerson's exhortation is longer, and he places it at the beginning of the third part of his *Opusculum tripartitum de preceptis decalogi, de confessione, et scientia mortis* (or as some versions have it *de arte moriendi*).

It is as follows: "Si veraces fidelesque amici cujuspiam egroti, curam diligentium agant pro ipsius vita corporali

[1] C. 11, c. 8.

[2] v. p. 102.

fragili et defectibili conservanda, exigunt a nobis multo fortius Deus et caritas pro salute sua spirituali sollicitudinem gerere specialem. In hac extrema necessitate mortis fidelis probatur amicus. Quippe nullum est opus misercordie majus sive commodius. Quod et tanti apud Deum meriti et amplioris frequenter estimatur, quemadmodum persone nostri Salvatoris Jesu Christi, si in terris nobiscum degeret impensum servitium corporale. Quamobrem cura fuit presenti scripto componere brevem quemdam exhortationis modum habendum circa eos qui sunt in mortis articulo constituti. Valentem etiam generaliter omnibus catholicis ad artem et notitiam bene moriendi conquirendam. Continet autem hoc opusculum breve quatuor particulas; scilicet exhortationes, interrogationes, orationes et obsecrationes."

THE CRAFT FOR TO DIE
TO THE HEALTH OF MAN'S SOUL

HERE BEGINNETH A LITTLE TREATISE SHORTLY COMPILED AND CALLED *ARS MORIENDI*: THAT IS TO SAY, THE CRAFT FOR TO DIE FOR THE HEALTH OF MAN'S SOUL

When any of likelihood[1] shall die, then it is most necessary to have a special friend, the which will heartily help and pray for him, and therewith counsel the sick for the weal of his soul; and moreover to see that all others so do about him, or else quickly for to make them depart.

Then is to be remembered the great benefits of God done for him unto that time, and specially of the passion of our Lord; and then is to be read some story of saints or the vii psalms with the litany or our Lady's psalter, in part or whole, with other. And ever the image of the crucifix is to be had in his sight, with other. And holy water is oftimes to be cast upon and about him for avoiding of evil spirits, the which then be full ready to take their advantage of the soul if they may.

And then and ever make him cry for mercy and grace, and for the help of our Blessed Lady and of

[1] *i.e.* is likely to.

other saints in whom afore he had a singular trust and love, and thereupon to make his prayers if he may.

When death cometh or any grievous pangs, or other great sickness, then prayer or devotion assuageth ; wherefore it is wisdom for one to pray afore any sickness come, and also when one may in his sickness, if he will not be deceived. So he is happy and may be glad that [at] such a time of most need [he] hath a faithful friend ; and that will say beside the prayers afore rehearsed, and cause other also to say devoutly in remembrance of the charity of Jesu Christ and of His passion, and for to have the rather[1] His mercy and help, iij Paternosters and iij Aves, with a Credo ; and therewith to exhort him, by a priest, or for need by another, in the manner as followeth :

Brother, or sister, remember well that God saith by His prophet and evangelist : Blessed be those that die and depart in our Lord, that is to say from the world and his pleasures, and die in the true faith of the church, and repentance for their sins. Sir, ye have great cause to be glad for to depart from this wretched world, and full of all misery ; and think that thee needs must depart, and desire heartily to be with Jesu Christ your Maker, Redeemer and Lord God, for He shall give to you now your inheritance that He did buy for you with His precious passion and blood. Wherefore this time of your departing shall be better to you than the time of your birth, for now all sickness, sorrow, and trouble shall depart now from you

[1] *i.e.* sooner.

for ever. Therefore be not aggrieved with your sickness and take it not with grutching, but take it rather by all gladness.

See at all times that ye be stable in your faith, and believe, and say your Credo, if that ye may—or else desire another heartily to do it for you here afore us openly. And arm you ever with the sign of the cross ✠ as a Christian man, for your defence against your ghostly enemies ; in the which doing God will be greatly pleased, and the rather take you for one of His folk, by protection and grace, and as His child of salvation.

Have ever a good and true belief, and nothing may be impossible unto you. And ever beware that ye fall not in despair, for that greatly would displease God, and can not be remedied. And remember the sins done aforetime shall never hurt you as to damnation, if they please you not now and that ye be sorry for them. *Saint Jerome* saith : If one should take his sickness or his death with grutching it is a token that he loveth not God sufficiently ; all is righteous that we suffer. Desire, with *Saint Austin*, of our Lord here to be cut with tribulation and to be burned with sickness and sorrow, so that ye may be saved hereafter for ever.

Now meek yourself and be sorry that ye have been so unkind to please and to keep His commandments, and presume not as of yourself any goodness, and say with all meekness thus : Good Lord, Jesu Christ, I knowledge that I have sinned grievously and by Thy grace I will gladly amend me if I should live. Have mercy now of me for Thy bitter passion.

Then ask him these questions following afore his death.

> Be ye glad that ye shall die in Christian belief? Let him answer: Yea.
>
> Know thee that ye hath not so well lived as ye should? Yea.
>
> Have ye will to amend if that ye should live? Yea.
>
> Believe ye that Jesu Christ, God Son of heaven, was born of Blessed Mary? Yea.
>
> Believe ye also that Jesu Christ died upon the cross to buy man's soul on Good Friday? Yea.
>
> Do ye thank God therefore? Yea.
>
> Believe ye that ye may not be saved but by His passion and death? Yea.

As long as the soul is in your body thank God for His death, and have a sure trust by it and His passion to be saved. And counsel him to say if he may these following words of great virtue:

> Put Christ's passion betwix me and mine evil works, and betwix me and His wrath. Now Lord God be merciful to me a sinner.
>
> The praise of Our Lord Jesu Christ, and the virtue of His passion, with the sign of the holy cross, and the undefiled virginity of Blessed Mary, His Mother, and the blessing of all saints, and the protection of all holy angels, with the

help and prayers of all saints, be betwix me and all mine enemies, now and in the hour of my death and departing. . AMEN.

Also these verses following be of great virtue in the time of death, and to be said by the sick if he may, or by another for him.

Dirupisti Domine vincula mea, tibi sacrificabo hostiam laudis, et nomen Domini invocabo. Deus propitius esto michi peccatori. Domine Jhesu Christe ego cognosco me graviter peccasse, et libenter volo me emendare per graciam tuam. Miserere mei propter amaram passionem tuam. Domine Jhesu, redemisti nos in sanguine tuo. Laus sit tibi pro amare passione tua. Largire clarum vespere, quo vita nusquam decidat : sed præmium mortis sacre perennis instet gloria.

Also to Our Lady :

Maria plena gracie, Mater misericordie, tu nos ab hoste protege, et in hora mortis suscipe.

And at last :

In manus tuas Domine commendo spiritum meum. In nomine patris, et filii, et spiritus sancti. AMEN.

HERE FOLLOWETH A SHORT AND SWEET REMEMBRANCE OF THF SACRAMENT OF THE ALTAR OR THAT IT BE RECEIVED OF THE SICK PERSON, OR ANY OTHER, AFORE THEIR COMMUNING

Welcome Blessed Jesu, my Lord God and Saviour, to whom is appropried all mercy and pity. Remember good Lord how frail my nature and substance is, and have mercy and pity on me, great sinner, after Thy great mercies and for Thy bitter passion. For I knowledge and believe faithfully, as a Christian child of Thine, that Thou here in form of bread is the same my Lord God that of Thy goodness came down from heaven, and was born and took my nature of Blessed Virgin Mary, and died for me, and rose the third day, and after ascended in to heaven, and there reigneth with the Father and the Holy Ghost and all saints, for ever immortal: the which for our great health, frailty, and daily transgression, and in remembrance of Thy great love and passion, hast ordained this Thy blessed Body in this wise to be taken of me, and of all other willing to be saved.

I know well that I am far unworthy to be called Thy child or servant, for the great multitude of my sins; howbeit Thou mayst make me rightful and able the which only of sinners hast made great saints of heaven. By that Thy great power and might grant me now to take Thee meekly, in all fear, and with wailing for my sins, and with a spiritual gladness. Come now, good Lord, into my heart and cleanse it of all sins. Enter into my soul and make it whole, and therewith sanctify me within and without, and be my defence for body and soul, rebuking and putting aside all mine enemies far from the presence of Thy power; that I then so defended by Thee, may have a free and sure passage to Thy kingdom, where I shall not see Thee in This form by mystery, but I shall see Thee face to face ; where I shall never hunger nor thirst, but ever be in joy with Thee and Thine, there to glorify Thee and to worship Thee, to laud and to praise Thee, world without end. AMEN.

BY THESE FOLLOWING ARE VENIAL SINS TAKEN AWAY ; IF THEY BE DONE DEVOUTLY

In taking holy water [and] holy bread ; also by saying of the Paternoster, spiritually, for this clause and petition : *Dimitte nobis debita nostra sicut et nos dimittimus debitoribus nostris* ; and also by knocking of the breast for one's sins ; and also for saying of *Deus propicius esto in peccatori* ; and by saying of the common *Confiteor* at mass or at other time. Also by receiving of any of the sacraments of the church, and specially of the Body of our Lord. Also by hearing of mass, and by the sight of the sacrament of the altar, there or elsewhere. By the blessing of a bishop or of a priest at his mass. By any of the deeds of mercy ; by pardons ; by martyrdoms and penance ; by forgiveness to a trespassour ; by good ensample giving, or by converting of others to good life ; by patient thanking in trouble, and by contrition for sins, with displeasure of them. And for every good deed doing with good entent and devotion. AMEN.

The Famous Doctor Johan Gerson, Chancellor of Paris, taking his ground from Holy Scripture, and according with holy doctors, saith thus :

> Our most merciful Father, Lord God, knowing our frailty and readiness to all sin, is ever ready during this wretched and mortal life, by many and diverse ways to forgive us ever our trespass and to grant and give us His grace ; if so be that truly we do ordain unto Him these iii virtues following, so that they be said and done with all the heart devoutly.
>
> The first is that thou shalt say : Blessed Lord, I knowledge that I have sinned grievously against Thy goodness thus and thus—rehearsing thy sins,—and I am displeased therewith, by reason of the which I do penance and will do ; for I know well that I have grieved the merciful Lord and broken Thy commandments, in the which Thou only ought to be worshipped.
>
> The second, say this : Good Lord, I have a good purpose and desire with Thy help to be right ware hereafter that I fall not into sin, and I entend to flee the occasions after the possibility of my power.
>
> The third is this : Gracious Lord, I have good will to make an whole confession of all my sins, when place and time convenient may be had, according to Thy commandments and all holy church.
>
> These three verities or truths whosoever

sayeth with his heart unfeigningly, in what place that ever he be, he may be sure that he is in the state of grace and salvation, and that he shall have everlasting life, though all he had done all the sins of the world. And if he deceased without any other confession for lack of a priest, as sleeping, or sudden death, he should be saved suffering and sore hard pain in purgatory. Wherefore it is good counsel that every Christian man once or twice on the day, early or late, or else at least on holy days, examine his conscience and remember if that he may with all his heart unfeigningly say these iij truths. And if he can so do he may be sure that he is in the state of grace; and if he may not, but is in will to sin again, and to have his delectation with deed, and will not flee the occasions of mortal sins, and so, drowned in sin, will not arise, such one may be certain that the Pope may not assoil him. Not for thy good it is that such one use much prayer and give alms, and (to) do other good deeds after their power, that God the rather may lighten their hearts and the sooner turn to goodness. AMEN.

NOTE ON CAXTON'S TRACT

This tract of Caxton's was found in the middle of a volume of black letter tracts in the Bodleian Library, and Mr Blades avers that "no other copy in any language, in print or manuscript, appears to be known."[1] It has no date, printer's name, or place, but it is in Caxton's No. 6 type, with a few lines in the No. 1 type of Wynkyn de Worde, who was Caxton's workman and successor. We may therefore infer that it was one of the last books printed by Caxton, or one of the first printed by de Worde. In either case it was probably issued from Caxton's House at Westminster, in 1491, the year of his death. Mr Nicholson the late librarian of Bodley's Library says "it does not answer to any of the three printed Latin treatises known as *Ars Moriendi* which the Bodleian possesses," but that "the heading of the treatise suggests that it was a translation of a work already known by a particular name; the name given is in Latin; and occasional turns of expression . . . suggest a Latin original for parts at least."[2]

I think it will be evident to anyone who reads these two tracts of Caxton's, after reading the longer version of *The Craft of Dying*, that Mr Nicholson was right about the Latin original, and that the latter must have been the *Speculum* or *Tractatus de arte Moriendi*; and also that this particular tract appears to be a further abridgment of Caxton's own already abridged version.

Only those parts of the Tract which have any reference to death are given here. The last pages contain: A singular prayer to be said at the Feast of the Dedication of any church, or at any other time; The twelve degrees of Humility; The seven degrees of Obedience; The seven degrees of Patience; and The fifteen degrees of Charity.

---

[1] *Biography and Typography of William Caxton* (1582), p. 359; but see appendix, p. 170.

[2] *See* Introductory Note to the facsimile issued by E. W. B. Nicholson, M.A., p. 5.

A CHAPTER TAKEN FROM THE OROLOGIUM SAPIENTIÆ

OROLOGIUM SAPIENTIÆ

HER SHOWETH THE FIFTH CHAPTER OF A TREATISE CALLED *OROLOGIUM SAPIENCIE* IN MANNER OF A DIALOGUE: AND TREATETH HOW WE SHALL LEARN TO DIE

HOW THE DISCIPLE OF EVERLASTING WISDOM SHALL CON[1] LEARN TO DIE FOR THE LOVE OF JESU

SINCE it is that death nought to man, but rather from him, taketh, and priveth him of that he hath, whereof profiteth this doctrine of death? Say me it seemeth wonderful, and therefore teach me heavenly master.

WISDOM

Thou shalt understand that it is a science most profitable, and passing all other sciences, for to con[2] die. For a man to know that he shall die, that is common to all men; as much as there is no man that may ever live or he hath hope or trust thereof; but thou shalt find full few that have this cunning to con to die. For that is a sovereign gift of God; sothly for a man to con to die is for to have his heart and his soul at all times upward to those things that be above; that is to say that what time death cometh

[1] be able to. [2] learn to.

it find him ready, so that he receive it gladly, without any withdrawing; right as he that bideth the desired coming of his well-beloved fellow. But alas, for sorrow thou shalt find among some religious, as well as in vain seculars, full many that hate so much the death that unneth[1] they will have it in mind, or hear speak thereof; for they would not go from this world. And the cause is for they learn not to con die. For they spend much of their time in vain speaking, playings, and in vain occupations and curiosities; and other such vain things. And therefore what time death cometh suddenly, for as much as he findeth them unready, he draweth out of the body the wretched soul and leadeth it to hell; as he would oftentimes have done to thee, had not the great mercy of God withstood him.

Wherefore leave you vain things to them that be vain, and give good intent to my doctrine; the which shall profit thee more than choice gold, and than the books of all the philosophers that have been. And [that] this doctrine of me may more fervently move thee, and that it be alway dwelling and fixed in thy mind, (and) therefore under a fellowable ensample, I shall give thee the mystery of this doctrine; the which shall profit thee greatly to the beginning of ghostly health, and to a stable fundament of all virtues.

See now therefore the likeness of a man dying and therewith speaking with thee.

And then the disciple hearing this began to gather

[1] scarcely.

all his wits from outward things, and in himself busily to consider and behold that likeness set before him; for then there appeared before him the likeness of a fair young man, the which was suddenly overcome with death in hasty time for to die, and had not disposed for the health of his soul before: the which with a careful[1] voice cried, and said:
CIRCUMDEDERUNT ME GENITUS MORTIS: DOLORES Ps. xvii. 5
INFERNI CIRCUMDEDERUNT ME. That is: the waymenting[2] of death hath umbelapped me,[3] and the sorrows of hell have environed me.

Alas, my God Everlasting, whereto was I born into this world, and why, after that I was born, had I not perished anon? For the beginning of my life was weeping and sorrow, and now the end and the passing is with great care and mourning. O death how bitter is thy mind[4] to a liking heart, and nourished up in delights! O how little trowed I that I should so soon die! But now thou, wretched death, suddenly lying in wait as a thief, hast fallen upon me. Now for sorrow, wringing mine hands, I yield out my groaning and yelling, desiring to flee death. But there is no place to flee from it. I look on every side and I find no counsellor nor comforter; for death is utterly fixed and set in me, and therefore it may not be changed. I hear that horrible voice of death saying to me in this manner: "Thou art the son of death; neither riches, nor reason, nor kinsmen, nor friends, may deliver thee from my

[1] sorrowful. [2] *i.e.* sighing, lamenting.
[3] enwrapped. [4] *i.e.* memory.

hand; for thy end is come, and it is deemed, and therefore it must be done."

O my God shall I now needs die? May not this sentence be changed? Shall I now so soon go from this world? O the great cruelty of death. Spare, I pray thee, to the youth, spare to the age that is not yet fully ripe. Do not so cruelly with me. Withdraw me not so unpurveyed[1] from the light of life.

The Disciple, hearing these words, turned to him and said:

Disciple

Friend thy words seem to me not savouring of discipline. Wot thou not that the doom of death is given to all men, for it taketh no person afore other and it spareth no man; and it hath no mercy neither of young nor old. It slayeth as well the rich as the poor; and sooth it is that right many, before the perfect fulfilling of their years, be drawn away from this life. Trowest thou that death should have shared thee alone? Nay, for the prophets be dead.

The Likness, or Image of Death, answered and said

Soothly, he said, thou art an heavy comforter for my words sound not to wisdom, but rather they be like to fools; the which have lived evil unto their death, and have wrought those things that be worthy

[1] *i.e.* unprovided.

death, and yet they dread not death when it nigheth them. They be blind, and like to unreasonable beasts that see not, before their last end, nor that that is to come after death. And therefore I weep not all for sorrowing of the doom of death, but I weep for the harms of undisposed death ; I weep not for I shall pass hence, but I am sorry for the harms of those days that be passed, the which unprofitably dispendeth without any fruit. ERRAVIMUS A VIA VERITATIS ET JUSTITIÆ LUMEN NON LUXIT NOBIS, etc. : *In libro Sapiencie*, Wisd. v. 6 sqq. Alas, how have I lived. I have erred from the way of soothfastness, and the light of righteousness hath not shined into me, nor the truth of understanding was not received in my soul. Alas what profiteth to me pride, or the boast of riches ; what hath that holpen me ? All those be passed as shadows and as the mind [1] of gests [2] of one day passing forth. And therefore is now my word and my speech in bitterness to my soul, and my words full of sorrow, and mine eyes deceived.

O why had not I been ware in my youth of this that falleth me in my last days, when I was clothed with strength and beauty, and had many years before me to come ; that I might have known the evils that have suddenly fallen upon me in this hour.

I took no force [3] to the worthiness of time, but freely [have] given me to lost and to wretched life, and spent my days all in vanities. And therefore, right as fishes be caught with the hook, and as birds

[1] *i.e.* memory. [2] deeds or actions.
[3] *i.e.* gave no heed to.

be taken with the grin,[1] so am I taken with cruel death that hath come upon me suddenly; and my time of life is passed and slidden away, and may not be cleped again[2] of no man. There was none hour so short but therein I might have gotten ghostly winnings that pass in value all earthly goods withouten comparison. Alas, I wretched, why have I dispended so many gracious days in most vain and long speaking, and so little force have taken of myself!

O the unspeakable sorrow of mine heart! Why have I so given me to vanities, and why in all my life learned I not to die! Wherefore all ye that be here and see my wretchedness, ye that be jocund in the flower of youth, and have yet time able to live, behold me and take heed of my mischieves[3] and sorrows, and eschew[4] your harm by my peril. Spend ye in God the flower of your youth, and occupy ye the time that is given you in holy works; lest that if ye do like to me, ye suffer the pains that I suffer.

O everlasting God, to Thee I knowledge, complaining the great wretchedness that I feel of the wanton youth in which I hated words of blaming for my trespasses. I would not obey to him that taught me, and turned away the ear from them that would goodly counsel me. And I hated discipline, and mine heart would not assent to blaming. And therefore now am I fallen into a deep pit, and am caught with the grin of death. It had been better to me if

[1] snare. [2] *i.e.* re-called.
[3] distresses or needs. [4] avoid, confess.

I had never been born, or else that I had perished in my mother's womb, than I had so unprofitably spent the time that was granted to me to do penance, and misused it so wretchedly in pride.

DISCIPLE

Lo, we all die: as water falleth down into the earth, and turneth not again. And God will not that man's soul perish, but withdraweth from him, that he be not fully lost that is of himself abject. Wherefore hear now my counsel. Repent ye of all thine offences, and do penance for thy misdeeds that be passed, and turn ye to thy Lord God by good deeds. For He is full benign and merciful: and if it so be that the end be good, it sufficeth to heal of soul.

THE IMAGE OF DEATH ANSWERED

What word is this that thou speakest? Shall I turn me and do penance? Seest thou not the anguish of death that overlieth me? Lo, I am so greatly feared with the dread and horror of death, and so bounden with the bonds of death, that I may not see nor know what I shall do. But right as the partridge constrained under the claws and nails of the hawk is half dead for dread, right so all vice[1] is gone from me; thinking not else but how I might in any wise escape this peril of death, the which nevertheless I may not escape.

O that blessed penance and turning from sin

[1] Douce 114 reads 'witte.'

be-times, for that is [the] sicker way. Forsooth he that hath late turned him and giveth him to penance, he shall be in doubt and uncertain, for he wot not whether his penance be true or feigned. Woe to me that hath so long suffered for to amend my life. Alas I have too long tarried for to get me heal. Lo all my days be passed and lost, and wretchedly been perished and gone so negligently that I wot not whether I have spent one day of them all in the will of God; and the exercises of all virtues not done so worthily and so perfectly as peraventure I might and should have done, or else if I ever did to my Maker so pleasant service and acceptable as mine estate asketh. Alas, for sorrow thus it is, wherefore all mine inward affections [have] been sore wounded. O God everlasting, how shameful shall I stand at the doom before Thee and all Thy saints, when I shall be compelled to give answer and reason of all that I have done and let undone. And what shall I say hereto, but at next[1] is my tribulation, then [when] I pass forth from this world. Take now heed of me I pray you busily. Lo, in this hour I would have more joy of a little short prayer, as of an *Ave Maria*, said devoutly of me, than a thousand pounds of silver or gold.

O my God, how many goods have I negligently lost. Soothly now know I that as [to] the greatness of heavenly needs, it should more have availed me a busy keeping of mine heart, and all my wits with cleanness of heart, than that I lost, or by inordinate

[1] *i.e.* the nearest or first thing.

affection defouled and defected,[1] that any other man thirty years had made him by prostrations, for to get me reward of God here or in bliss.

O ye all that see my wretchedness, have compassion on me, and have mercy on yourself; and while your strength suffices and have time, help and gather to heavenly barns heavenly treasures, the which may receive you into everlasting tabernacles, what time that ye fail; and that ye be not left void in such an hour that is to come to you, as ye see me void now and of all goods dispoiled.

Disciple

My loved friend I see well that thy sorrow is full great, and therefore I have compassion of thee with all mine heart; adjuring thee by God Almighty that thou give me counsel whereby that I may be taught, that I fall not in such peril of undisposed death.

Hereto said the Image of Death

The counsel of sovereign prudence and most providence standeth in this point, that thou dispose thee, while thou art whole and strong, by true contrition and clean and whole confession, and by due satisfaction; and all wicked and noyous things, that should withdraw or let thee from everlasting health, that thou cast away from thee; and that thou keep thee so in all times as [though] thou should pass out of this world, this day, or to-morrow, or at

[1] *i.e.* made defective or dishonoured.

the uttermost within this sen'night. Put[1] in thine heart as though thy soul were in purgatory and had in penance for thy trespass ten years in the furnace of the burning fire, and only this year is granted thee for thine help; and so behold often sithes thy soul among the burning coals, crying:

"O Thou best beloved of all Friends, help Thy wretched soul! Have mind on me, that am now in so hard prison. Have mercy on me that stand[2] all desolate, and suffer me no longer to be tormented in this dark prison. For I am forsaken of this world. There is none that showeth me kindness, or that would put to [a] hand to help me, needy. All men seek their own profit and have forsaken me, and left me in this painful burning flame and desolate."

[The] Disciple answered

Soothly this doctrine of thine were most profitable, whoso hath it by experience as thou hast. But though it so be, that thy words be seen full stirring and biting, nevertheless they profit little as to many folk, for they turn away their face that they will not see unto their end. Their eyes see not, nor their ears hear not. They weened to live long, and that deceiveth them; and for they dread not undisposed[3] death, therefore they take no keep of seeing to-fore the harms thereof, what time that the messenger of death cometh;—that is to say hard and great sickness.

[1] *i.e.* consider or ponder. [2] *i.e.* remain, or am.
[3] *i.e.* unprepared.

Then come friends and fellows to the sick man for to visit him and comfort him. And then all proffer and behote[1] good things; and that him need not to dread the death, and that there is no peril thereof, and that it is but a runniug of humours unkindly, or stopping of the sinews or the veins, that shall soon pass over.

Thus the friends of (the) bodies be enemies to (the) souls. For what time the sickness continually increaseth, and he that is sick trusteth ever of amendment, at the last suddenly he falleth and without fruit of heal yieldeth up the wretched soul; right so these that hear thy words—the which beleven[2] all together to man's prudence and worldly wisdom—they cast behind their backs thy words, and will not obey (to) thy healthful counsel.

The Image of Death said

Therefore what time they be taken with the grin of death, when there falleth upon them suddenly tribulation and anguish, they shall cry and not be heard; forasmuch as they had Wisdom in hate, and despised to hear my counsel. And right as now full few be found that be compunctious through my words for to amend them and turn their life into better, so forsooth—for the malice of the fiend in this time, and default of ghostly fervour, and the wickedness of the world, now in his eld,[3] letteth him—so that there be but few so perfectly disposed[4] to death: the which for great abstraction from the

[1] promise. [2] *i.e.* trust. [3] old age. [4] prepared.

world and devotion of heart, coveting to die for the desire of everlasting life, and within all his inward affection desiring to be with Christ ;—but rather the contrary. And for the most part of people,—they be suddenly with bitter death overcome that they be found at that time all undisposed in manner ; as I am now overcome.

And if thou wilt know the cause of so great and so common a peril, lo, it is the inordinate desire of worship[1] and the superfluous care of the body. Earthly love, and too much busyness about worldly living, blinds many hearts of the commonalty, and brings them at the last to these mischieves. But soothly if thou, with few, desirest to be saved from the peril of undisposed death hear my counsel, and oft sithes set before thine eyes this that thou seest now in my sorrowful person, and busily bring it to thy mind ; and thou shalt find soon that my doctrine is to thee most profitable. For thou hast so [much] profit thereby that, not only thou shalt not dread to die, but also (the) death—that is to all living men dreadful,—thou shalt abide and receive with desire of thine heart, in that it is the end of travail and the beginning of the felicity of everlasting joy. This thing look thou do : that thou every day bring me inwardly to thy mind, and busily take tent[2] to my words, and sadly[3] write them in thy heart. Of the sorrows and anguish that thou seest in me take heed, and think upon those things that be to come in hasty[4]

[1] *i.e.* honour.
[2] care or heed.
[3] constantly.
[4] *i.e.* sudden.

time upon thee. Have mind of my doom, for such shall be thy doom.

O how blessed art thou, ARSENIE, that ever had this hour of death before thine eyes! And so blessed is he, the which wot what time his Lord cometh and knocketh on the gate, and findeth him ready to let Him in. For by what manner of death he be overlaid, he shall be purged and brought to the sight of Almighty God; and, in the passing of his spirit, it shall be received into the blessed palace of everlasting bliss.

But woe is me, wretched! Where trowest thou shalt abide this night my spirit? Who shall receive my wretched soul, and where shall it be harboured at night in that unknown country? Oh how desolate thou shalt be, my soul, and abject, passing all other souls! Therefore, having compassion on myself among these bitter words, I shed out tears as the river. But what helpeth it to weep or to multiply many bitter words? It is concluded and may not be changed.

O my God, now I make an end of my words. I may no longer make sorrow, for lo, now is the hour come that will take me from the earth. Woe is me now! I see and know that I may no longer live, and that death is at next.[1] For lo, the hands unwieldy begin to rancle,[2] the face to pale, the sight to deceive, and the eyes to go in. The light of the world I shall no more see, and the estate of another world, before the eyes of my soul, in my mind, I

[1] *i.e.* directly at hand. O.E.D. [2] fester.

begin to hold. O my God, how dreadful a sight is this! Lo, the cruel beasts and the horrible faces of devils, and black forshapen things withouten number have environed me, a-spying and abiding my wretched soul—that shall in haste pass out—if peradventure it shall be taken to them for to be tormented, as for her bote.[1]

O thou most righteous Doomsman, how strait and hard be thy dooms; charging[2] and hard deeming me, wretched, in those things the which few folk charge or dread, forasmuch as they seem small and little. O the dreadful sight of the righteous Justice, that is now present to me by dread, and suddenly to come in deed. Lo, (the) death, swift perishing[3] the members, is come, that witnesseth the kind[4] of the flesh that perisheth and overcometh the spirit.

Now farewell, fellows and friends most dear: for now in my passing I cast the eyes of my mind into purgatory, whither that I shall now be led, and out thereof I shall not pass till I have yielded the last farthing of my debt for sin. There I behold with the eye of mine heart wretchedness and sorrow, and manifold pain and tormenting. Alas, me wretched! There I see—among other pains that longen to that place—rising up flames of fire, and the souls of wretched folk cast therein; up and down, to and fro, that run as sparks of fire in midst of that burning fire: right as in a great town, all one fire. And in the fire and in the smoke the sparks be borne up and

[1] remedy.
[2] accusing.
[3] *i.e.* causing to perish, destroying.
[4] nature.

down. So the souls, waymenting for sorrow of their pains, cry everyone and say these words: MISEREMINI MEI, MISEREMINI MEI, SALTUM VOS, ETC. Have mercy on me, have mercy on me, at the last, ye that be my friends. Where is now the help of my friends? Where be now the good behests of our kinsmen and others; by whose inordinate affection we took no force[1] of ourselves, and so increased we this pain to ourselves. Alas, why have we done so? Lo the least pain of this purgatory that we now feel passeth all manner of jewesses[2] of that temporal world; the bitterness of pain that we now feel in one hour, seemeth as great as all the sorrows of the passing world in an hundred years. But passing[3] all other torments and pains, it grieveth me most the absence of that blessed Face of God.

These words that I have here now said in my last passing I leave to thee as a mind: and so passing I die.

At this vision the disciple made great sorrow, and for dread all his bones quaked. And then turning him to God he said:

DISCIPLE

Where is everlasting Wisdom? Now Lord hast Thou forsaken me, Thy servant. Thou wouldest teach me wisdom enough, but I am almost brought to the death. O my God, how much bindeth me the presence of death that I have seen! Now the

[1] *i.e.* heed. [2] *i.e.* extortioners. [3] *i.e.* surpassing.

Image of Death hath so overlaid all my mind that unnethes [1] wot I whether I have seen the Image of Death or not; for I am so greatly astonied that unnethes wot I whether this that I have seen be so in deed, or in likeness. O Lord of Lords, dreadful and merciful, I thank Thee with all mine heart of Thy special grace, and I behote [2] amendment, for I am made afeared with passing great dread.

Ah forsooth! I never perceived in my life the perils of undisposed death so openly as I have now in this hour. I believe for certain that this dreadful sight shall avail to my soul for ever. For certain now, I know, that we have not here none everlasting city, and therefore to the unchangeable state of the soul that is to come, I will dispose me with all my might. And I purpose me to learn to die. And I hope by God's grace to amend my life withouten any withdrawing or differing; [3] for sithen I am made so sore afeared so only to the mind, what should be to me the presence thereof? Wherefore now do away for me the softness of bedding, and the preciosity of clothing, and the sloth of sleep, and all that letteth me from my Lord Jesu Christ.

O Thou Holy and merciful Saviour put [4] me not to bitter death. Lo, I falling down before Thee, with weeping tears ask of Thee that Thou punish me here at Thy will, so that there Thou receive [5] not my wicked deeds into the last end; for soothly in that

[1] scarcely. [2] promise. [3] *i.e.* disputing.
[4] *i.e.* give. [5] *i.e.* admit.

horrible place there is so great sorrow and pain that no tongue may suffer to tell.

O how great a fool have I been unto this time, in-so-much as I have so little force taken of undisposed death, and the pain of purgatory that is so great. And how great wisdom it is to have these things oft before thine eyes. But now that I am so ferdly[1] monished and taught, I open mine eyes and dread it greatly.

Wisdom answering and said

These things that be said, my Son, in all times have in mind, while thou art whole, young, and mighty, and mayst amend thyself. But what time thou comest to that hour, in soothness and none otherwise may thou help thyself; then is there none other remedy but that thou commit thee to the mercy of God only; and that thou take My passion betwixt thee and My doom, lest that thou dread My right-eousness more than needeth—for so thou might fall down from thine hope. And now, forasmuch as thou art afeard with a passing dread, be of good comfort; understanding that the dread of God is the beginning of wisdom. Seek thy books, and thou shalt find how many goods and profits the mind of death bringeth to man. Wherefore have mind of thy Creator and Eccl. xii. 1.
Maker in the days of thy youth, or that the powder turn again into his earth, whence he came from, and the spirit turn again to the Lord that gave it him. And bless thou God of Heaven with all thine heart,

[1] fearfully.

and be kind to him that giveth thee grace to see this. For there be full few that perceive with their heart the unstableness of this time; nor [the] deceit of death, that in all times lieth in a-wait, nor the everlasting felicity of that country which is to come. Lift up your eyes and look about thee busily, and see how many there be blind in their souls, and close their eyes, that they look not unto their last end, and stop their ears, that they hear not for to be converted and healed of sin. And therefore their loss and damnation shall not long tarry, but if they amend.

Also behold the company without number of them that be now lost through the mischief of undisposed death. Number the multitude of them, if thou may, and take heed how many there be the which in thy time, dwelling with thee, now be dead and passed hence from this earth. How great a multitude of brethren and fellows, and others of thy knowledge, in so few years be gone before thee—that art yet a young man and left yet on life—and they be dead. Ask of them all, and seek of everyone; and they shall teach thee and answer to thee, weeping and moaning, saying thus: O how blessed is he that seeth before, and purveyeth for these last things; and keepeth him from sin, and doeth after thy counsel; and in all time disposeth him to his last home.

Wherefore putting a-back all things that shall withdraw thee here-from, ordain for thine house, and make thee ready to that last way of every man, and to the hour of death;—for in certain thou wottest not in what hour it shall come, and how nigh it is. And therefore, right as a travelling man, standing in the haven, beholdeth busily a ship that swiftly saileth toward far countries that he should go to, lest that it should overpass him he standeth still and removeth not thence till it come to him ; right so stand thou stably in virtues, and more for love and for dread, so that thy life and all thy working be dressed and set to that intent : ever principally to love and please thy Lord God, turning to His mercy so that thou have a blessed obit.[1] By the which thou mayst at the last come to thy place of immortality and everlasting felicity. Amen.

NOTE ON THE OROLOGIUM SAPIENTIÆ

This chapter is a transcription from the Douce MS. 322 (fol. 20) and is also found in MS. Harl. 1706 (fol. 20);—these two manuscripts being in many respects very similar, although the Harleian MS. contains much that is not in the Douce MS. Another translation of this chapter—which I have not seen noted elsewhere—is in MS. Bod. 789 (fol. 123) under the heading: "The most profitable sentence to deadly men in the which they may learn to know to die." It begins : "To kunne deie is to have the herte and the soule," etc. This manuscript dates from the beginning of the fourteenth century and is therefore earlier than the Douce MS. Another more complete version of the

[1] *i.e.* death.

Horologium, containing seven chapters, is found in the Douce MS. 114 (fol. 117).[1] This was printed by Caxton in 1490, under the title: The seuen points of the Wisdom, or Orologium Sapientiæ." There is also a French translation of these "seuen chapters," in a fifteenth-century manuscript in the British Museum (Harl MS. 43869), which is nearly twice as long as the English text.

The *Orologium Sapientiæ* has frequently and quite mistakenly been ascribed to Richard Rolle. It is of course by Henry Suso, although Dr Horstmann's statement that it is an "English reproduction of Heinrich Suso's *Buch von der göttlichen Weisheit* is also misleading.[2] In reality Suso translated his own *Büchlein der ewigen Weisheit* into Latin under the title *Horologium Sapientiæ*, and in thus doing added to it so considerably as to make it almost a new book.

Suso, who took his mother's name, his father being Herr von Berg, was born in 1300 at Überlingen near Lake Constance. He came under Eckart's influence when studying theology at Cologne, where he wrote his most mystical treatise, *Das büchlein der Wahrheit*. After wandering through Suabia as a preacher he settled at Ulm about 1348. It was there that he wrote these later books in which he discusses the more practical aspects of mysticism. Suso has been called the poet of the early mystic movement, the "Minnesinger of *Gottesminne*"; he is purely medieval in tone, though inspired by the romanticism of the age of chivalry. He died at Ulm in 1366.

[1] *cf.* Anglia, vol. x. p. 323.
[2] *cf.* Library of English Writers, vol. ii. p. xliii.

THREE FRAGMENTS WHICH TEACH A MAN FOR TO DIE

HERE SHOWETH A CHAPITLE TAKEN OUT OF A BOOK CLEPED TOURE OF ALL TOURES: AND TEACHETH A MAN FOR TO DIE

AGAINST his will he dieth that hath not learned to die. Learn to die and thou shalt con[1] to live, for there shall none con to live that hath not learned to die; and he shall be cleped a wretch that cannot live and dare not die.

If thou wilt live freely learn to die wilfully;[2] and if thou ask of me how many it learneth, I shall tell it thee anon.

Thou shalt understand that this life is not else but death; for death is a passing as every man knoweth well. Wherefore men say of a man when he dieth that he passeth; and when he is dead he is passed. This life is not but only a passing, yea, forsooth, and that a full short passing. For all the life of a man's youth—if he lived a thousand year—were not as a moment in regard to the other life that ever shall last; other in joy withouten end, other in torment everlasting. This witnesseth to us well earls, kings, and emperors, which some time had the joy of this

[1] *i.e.* learn. [2] *i.e.* willingly.

world, and now in hell wallowing and weeping, crying and saying: Alas, what is now worth to us our power, honour, noblesse, joy, and boasts! Sooner it is passed than the shadow. For as the shot of an arblaster[1] passeth, right so passeth our life. Now be we born, and now be we dead anon; and all our life is not a moment. Now we be in torment everlasting: our joy is turned into weeping, carols to sorrow, garlands, robes, games, feasts, and all goods to us be fallen. Such be the songs of hell. And Holy Writ telleth us that this life is not but a passage, and for to live is not but for to pass. Then for to live is not but for to die, and that is sooth as the Paternoster. For when thou beginnest for to live, anon thou shalt begin for to die: and all thine age and thy time that is passed, death hath it conquered and holdeth.

Thou sayest that thou hast now forty years. That is not sooth. The death hath them, and never shall they thee hold.

Therefore is the wit of this world folly. These clerks see not this thing; and yet day and night they do this thing. And the more that they [have] it done, the less they it know: for alway they die, and yet con they not die. For day and night diest thou, as I have to thee said; yet in another manner I shall teach thee this clergy,[2] that thou con die well and live well.

Now hearken and understand. Death is not else but a departing of the body and of the soul, as every

[1] cross-bowman. [2] *i.e.* clerical learning or skill.

man knoweth. Now teacheth us the wise man, CATON. Learn we, he sayeth, for to die. Depart we the spirit from the body. Oft so die the great philosophers, that this life so much hated, and this world so much dispraised—and so much desired the death, that they fell down by their own will: but that was to them little worth for they had not the grace nor the truth of Jesu Christ.

But these holy men, that loved and dreaded God, that out of three deaths hath passed. Twain, for they be dead unto sin, and dead unto the world; and they abiden the third death, that is departing of the body and the soul. Betwix them and paradise is not but a little wall, which they pass through thought and desiring. And if the body be on this half, the heart and the spirit is on the other half. There they have (the) conversation, as Saint Paul saith: their place, their joy, their comfort and their desiring. And therefore they hate this life that is but death, and desire the bodily death.

Death unto the good man is end of all evils, and entry and gates of all goods. Death is the running brook that departed from (the) life. Death is on this half, and life is on the other half. But the wise men of this world (that) on this half on the running brook see so clearly, and on that other half see not—and therefore Holy Writ clepeth them fools and blind. For this death they clepen life, and the death that these good men beginning of life, they clepen the end. And therefore they hate so much (the) death that they wot not what it is; nor beyond the running brook they have not dwelled. And he can nought[1] that goeth not out.

Then, if thou wilt wit what is good and what is evil, [cast out the world and learn to die. Depart thy body from thy soul through thought, send thine heart into that other world, that is into heaven, into hell, and into purgatory. And then thou shalt see what is good and what is evil].[2]

In hell thou shalt see more sorrow than man may devise. In purgatory more torment than man may endure. In paradise more joy than man may desire. Hell will teach thee how God shall venge deadly sin. Purgatory will show thee how God shall venge venial sin. In paradise thou shalt see aptly virtues and good works rewarded highly.

In these three things standeth what behoveth for to con well for to live, and well for to die.

[1] *i.e.* knows nothing.

[2] Omitted in Harl. 1706, probably because of the repetition of 'what is evil.'

THIS FOLLOWS *THE CRAFT OF DYING* IN MS. BOD. 423

HAVE in mind that thou hast one God that made thee of nought; which hath given thee thy right wits, thy right limbs, and other worldly ease, more than to another, as thou mayst see all day—which live in much disease and great bodily mischief.[1]

Think also how sinful thou art, and were [it] not the keeping of that good Lord God, thou shouldst fall into all manner of sin, by thine own wretchedness; and then thou mayst think soothly as of thyself there is none more sinful than thou art.

Also if thou have any virtue or grace of good living, think it cometh of God's fonde[2] and nothing of thyself. Think also how long and how oft God hath suffered thee in sin. He would not take thee into damnation when thou had deserved it, but gladly hath abiden thee till thou wouldst leave sin and turn thee to goodness; for loth Him were to forsake that He bought full sore with bitter pains. And, for He would not lose thee, He became man, born of a maiden, suffering great passion and death to save thee.

[1] ill, or need. [2] *i.e.* source.

HERE FOLLOW FOUR PROFITABLE THINGS TO HAVE IN MIND: WHICH BEEN HAD OUT OF THE THIRD CHAPTER OF A DEVOUT TREATISE AND A FORM OF LIVING;[1] THAT RYCHARDE HAMPOLE WROTE TO A DEVOUT PERSON IN THIS MANNER WISE

The first is the measure of thy life here; that is so short that unnethes it is nought;[2] for we live in a point—that is the least thing that may be—and soothly our life is less than a point if we liken it to the life that lasteth ever.

Another is uncertainty of our ending; for we wit never when we shall die, nor how we shall die, nor whither we shall go when we be dead; and that God will that it be uncertain to us, for He wills that we alway be ready to die.

The third is that we shall answer before the righteous Judge of all, the time that we have been here. How we have here lived, what our occupation hath been, and why; and what good we might have

[1] It is from chap. iv. of *The Form of Living*. *Cf.* Dr Hodgson's edit., p. 24, or Horstman, i. 19.

[2] *i.e.* scarcely is it anything.

done, while we have been idle. Therefore the prophet said : He hath cleped the time against me ; that is, each day He hath lent us here, for to spend in good use here, and in penance, and in God's service. If we waste it in earthly love and vanities, full grievously may we be deemed and punished. Therefore it is one of the most sorrows that may be, but[1] we enforce us namely in the love of God, and do good to all that we may, the while that our short time lasteth. And each time that we think not on God, we may account it as the time that we have lost.

The fourth is that we think how much that the joy is that they shall have which last and endure in God's love into their ending ; for they shall be brethren and fellow with angels and holy men, loving and having praising, and seeing the King of Joy, in the fairhead and the shining of His majesty ; the which sight shall be meat and all delights that any creature may think, and more than any man may tell to all his lovers withouten end. It is much lighter to come to that bliss than to tell it.

Also think what sorrow, and what pain and what torment, that they shall have the which loved not God over all other things that men see in this world ; but fill their body and their souls in lust and liking of this life, in pride and covetuousness and other sins. They shall burn in the fire of hell with the devil whom thy serve, as long as God is in heaven with His servants : that is evermore.

[1] unless.

NOTE ON THE TOWER OF ALL TOWERS

This fragment is taken from the Douce MS. 322 (fol. 25*b*). It follows the *Orologium Sapientiæ*, and immediately precedes *The Craft of Dying*. I have not been able to trace the book "cleped toure of all toures." Tower of all towers is probably a name for Heaven, and it may possibly be a translation from some Latin original. Perhaps someone who reads this may be able to throw light upon it. The Harleian MS. 1706 also contains a copy of the same fragment.

The other two fragments are from the Bodleian MS. 423. They are not contained in either the Douce or Rawlinson manuscripts.

THE LAMENTATION OF THE DYING CREATURE

THE LAMENTATION OF THE DYING CREATURE

THE DYING CREATURE ENSET WITH SICKNESS INCURABLE SORROWFULLY COMPLAINETH HIM THUS

ALAS that ever I sinned in my life. To me is come this day the dreadfullest tidings that ever I heard. Here hath been with me a sergeant of arms whose name is CRUELTY,[1] from the King of all Kings, Lord of all Lords, and Judge of all Judges; laying on me the mace of His office, saying unto me: I arrest thee and warn thee to make thee ready, and that thou fail not to be ready in every hour when thou be called on; thou shalt not wit when. And call sadly to thine remembrance thine old and [long][2] continued offences; and the goodness of God, how largely He hath departed[3] with thee the gifts of nature, the gifts of fortune, and the gifts of grace. And how He hath departed with thee largely and ordained thee at thy baptism three borrows,[4] that thou shouldest safely and surely be kept in thy tender age

[1] All words printed in capitals are written in red in the MS.

[2] Additions in square brackets are from Wynkyn de Worde's printed version.

[3] divided.

[4] *i.e.* sureties.

as well from vices as bodily peril; and ordained thee a good angel to keep and counsel thee—if thou have been counselled by him, bethink thee—and when thou camest to years of discretion he ordained thee three sad counsellors; REASON, DREAD, and CONSCIENCE. If thou have ruled thee by their counsel, call that to thy remembrance.

He ordained thee also five [WITS] servants, that thou shouldest be master of, and rule them after thy discretion; that is to say, thy sight, thy hearing, thy speech, thy feeling, and thy taste. How hast thou ruled those that be under thine obedience? Me seemeth thou hast much things to answer for. The Judge that shall sit upon thee, He will not be partial, nor He will not be corrupt with goods, but He will minister to thee justice and equity certainly as well as these three were. Certain things He forbade thee, and those things thou shouldest flee in every wise. There is, to wit, the SEVEN deadly sins; and all things that should provoke, move, or stir thereto, He bade thee flee. Hast thou done so? Hast thou kept His commandments TEN: and yet that is but a little thing.

THE LAMENTATION OF THE DYING CREATURE

Alas! alas! Excuse me I can not, and whom I might desire to speak for me I wot not. The day and time is so dreadful; the Judge is so rightful; mine enemies be so evil; my kin, my neighbours, my friends, my servants, be not favourable to me; and I wot well they shall not be heard there.

The Complaint of the Dying Creature to the Good Angel

O my Good Angel, to whom our Lord took me to keep, where be thee now? Me thinketh ye should be here, and answer for me; for the dread of death distroubleth me, so that I cannot answer for myself. Here is my bad angel ready, and is one of my chief accusers, with legions of fiends with him. I have no creature to answer for me. Alas it is an heavy case!

The Answer of the Good Angel to the Dying Creature

As to your bad deeds, I was never consenting. I saw your natural inclination more disposed to be ruled by your bad angel than by me. Howbeit, ye cannot excuse you, but when ye were purposed to do anything that was contrary to the commandments of God, I failed not to remember you that it was not well; and counselled thee to flee the place of peril, and the company that should stir or move you thereto. Can ye say nay hereto? How can ye think that I should answer for you?

The Complaint of the Dying Creature to Reason, Dread, and Conscience

O ye Reason, Dread, and Conscience, ye were assigned to be of my counsel. Now come, I require you, and help me to answer for me. For my defaults be so many, and so abominable in the sight of Him that shall be my Judge, and mine accusors so many and so unfriendly, that they leave not one fault behind. Now come, I require you, and help to answer for me, for it was never so great need. The fear and the dread that I am in distroubleth me so that one word I cannot speak for my life. Alas that ever I saw this day!

The Answer of Reason to the Dying Creature

Be not ye remembered that Our Lord ordaineth you a good angel and a bad angel; and He ordained you reason and discretion to know good from evil. He put you in free choice whether ye would do well or evil; and also commanded you to do good and leave the evil. Ye ought to call to your remembrance how well God hath done for you, and holpen you in every danger and peril: He would have been beloved, dreaded, and served, according to the manifold mercies and kindnesses that He hath showed unto you. How to answer for you I wot not. Loth I am to accuse you, and excuse you I can not.

The Complaint of the Dying Creature to Dread

O Dread, where be ye? Is there none help and succour with you to speak for me when I shall come to judgment?

THE ANSWER OF DREAD

No certainly. For when ye were set on pleasure and delectation of the world, REASON put in your mind that ye did not well, and I, DREAD, was with you at all times and in every place; and failed not to speak to you and to put you in mind of the shame of the world, dread of damnation, and of the peril that would follow—as well here as elsewhere—remembering[1] unto you the punishments that our Lord ordained for sin; saying to you: See ye not how graciously our Lord hath called you away from sin and wretchedness, if ye would understand it. How hath He long kept you in worship, estate, and in prosperity, and (ye) coude not[2] know the goodness of God. How hath He chastised you, and how oft; by loss of your children, loss of your kin, friends, and goods, and loss of all those things that ye be not pleased with; and set you in the indignation of high and mighty princes, and holp you out of the dangers and perils that ye have been in at all times; and yet have ye not loved Him and served Him, that in all these perils hath preserved and kept you, and hath been so gracious and good Lord to you. Who should speak for you. I? Nay certainly.

THE COMPLAINT OF THE DYING CREATURE TO CONSCIENCE

Alas, CONSCIENCE, is there no help with you? I have heard say, long ago, the world was evil to trust,

[1] de Worde, 'rehearsing.' [2] ye were not able to.

but I would hope that CONSCIENCE would have compassion of my distress ; and much the more that I am friendless.

THE ANSWER OF CONSCIENCE TO THE DYING CREATURE

I am sorry to accuse you, and excuse you I cannot. For CONSCIENCE and DREAD have been full seldom from you in every time and place of peril, and bad you flee the occasions of sin. Ye might have fled at that time, and would not. Now ye would flee Death, and can not. We should speak for you, and dare not ; and though we would, it availeth not. Ye must sorrowfully and meekly suffer the judgments that ye have deserved.

THE COMPLAINT OF THE DYING CREATURE TO THE FIVE WITS

O ye FIVE that were ordained to be my servants, and under mine obedience, and to have been ruled at all times as I would have you ; is there no good word that ye may say for me, and record my demeaning [1] to you, and report how I have ruled and governed you that were taken [2] me to keep, rule, and govern. Me seemeth ye should say for me now. Who might say so well for me as ye FIVE ? Ye have been continually with me ever sith I was born, night and day, and never at no time from me. Me thinketh of your kindness ye should have compassion on me, and say the best that ye coude say for

[1] demeanour. [2] *i.e.* given.

me. I have been friendly to you, and brought you in every place of pleasaunce and disport. Now show your kindness again to me and speak to FAITH and HOPE for me, that they would charitably do my message unto the most glorious Prince that ever was, is, or ever shall be.

THE ANSWER OF THE FIVE WITS

Certainly we marvel that ye will desire us to speak, for you understand those worshipful people hath denied and refused to speak for you ; your GOOD ANGEL, REASON, DREAD, and CONSCIENCE. How should ye be heard ? Or what credence will be given unto us that have been your servants and under your obeisance, and nothing done all times but as ye have commanded us to do ? Call to your remembrance how you ruled us Five, SIGHT, HEARING, FEELING, TASTING and SMELLING. Ye have at all times brought us in places of pleasance and disport ; and though it were disport and pleasance for the time, it is now sorrow, weeping, and wailing for your sake, that we cannot excuse you nor anything say for you that might be your weal or to your ease. For we have been privy and partners to all that hath been mis-done in any wise, and in every place. And our offence in all things is in your default. For, and ye had sadly[1] ruled us as a sovereign should, ye should have restrained in us every vice. For we should have been ruled by you in every thing ; and otherwise than ye

[1] wisely.

would have had us do, we would not have done. Therefore of your necessity your defaults must be laid upon you, for we have done as servants should do; and obeyed you in every thing, and disobeyed you in nothing. Wherefore of right the peril must be yours. What credence then would be given to us if we should say well for you? The people would say that we were false dissimulers,[1] and favourers of sin.

The Lamentation of the Dying Creature

Alas, there is no creature that I can complain me to but utterly refuseth to say anything that might be to my comfort.

The Complaint of the Dying Creature to Faith and Hope

O holy Faith and Hope, in you is all my trust. For how grievously, how mischievously[2] that ever I offended God, you displeased I never. I have alway believed as the Church of Christendom hath taught me; and specially of the most holy Incarnation I was never in doubt. I have believed in the most holy and glorious Trinity, the Father, the Son, and the Holy Ghost, three Persons; and They three but one God. I have believed in the second Person of the Trinity, descended into the bosom of the most pure, glorious, chaste, and meek Virgin, that ever was, is, or shall be; and medled[3] His very Godhead with her pure, chaste, virginity and maidenhead; and

[1] *i.e.* dissemblers. [2] wickedly. [3] *i.e.* mingled.

in her bosom was perfectly contained very God and Man, by the great mystery of the Holy Ghost, without knowledge and company of any earthly man, and she a pure, chaste, virgin, flowering in virginity, and by hearing of the holy Archangel Gabriel, which brought unto her the most gracious and good tidings that ever came to mankind.

Now holy FAITH, take with you HOPE, and ye twain, of your perfect charity, be mine advocates in the High Court, and refuse me not; nor disdain me for mine horrible and abominable sins that I have done, which asketh vengeance in this world, and damnation eternal, without the mercy of Him that is Almighty. What mean[1] might I have thereto? I pray you counsel me, for ye know well that my reason never discorded from the faith.

And as to you HOPE, I hope that ye will say for me that I have hoped always to the mercies of Almighty God; and that I should be one of the children of salvation, and one of those that should be redeemed by the precious and bitter painful passion, as other sinners have been. And certainly other plea or resistance I can not make. But, and ye twain would be mean for me to that most glorious and pure chaste Virgin, that chosen was by the one assent of the whole glorious Trinity to do the most glorious and worshipfullest act that ever was done. For her chastity, her pure virginity, her meekness, her virtue and her constancy, was cause that she was chosen by all the whole glorious Trinity to be the Daughter,

[1] mediator.

Mother, and Spouse to the most glorious Trinity; and that she should bear Him that should redeem all mankind from damnation. Who may so well (be) advocatrice to the Father, the Son, and the Holy Ghost as she? And ye will be mean to her for me, I hope she will not refuse me. For I understand and know well that she hath holpen many a sinner that hath right grievously offended; and in the holy psalm that was made between her and her cousin, Saint Elizabeth, it was said that all generations should bless her. I hope at the beginning of the world Our Lord put not me out of His number of those that should bless His most holy Mother, and record her mercy, pity, and grace that she showeth to sinners when they have none other succour nor help.

She is Mother of orphans, and she is Consolation of those that be desolate. She is Guide to those that be out of the way, to set them in the right way. I am an orphan. I am desolate. I am out of the way. I wot not where to cry and call after succour and help, but only to her that bare our aller[1] Redemptor. Who may so well be mean to the Son as the Mother? And ye twain, FAITH and HOPE, would be mean to the Mother of mercy for me. Now gracious FAITH and HOPE, do your part, and disdain not my request though I desire you to this occupation. For, and ye twain would deny me, to say for me, I doubt I should fall in despair. For on whom to call for after succour I wot not; and to put myself in press[2] as a poor naked beast, unclothed in virtue and repleted with

[1] *i.e.* of us all. [2] *i.e.* exert myself.

vices, naked of grace and in mine own default ; and to come to the presence of the King of all Kings, (and) unpurveyed of[1] all things that would accord with His most royal and imperial estate ;—I dare not take it upon me. I should be in such dread and fear that I should not come, nor dare speak for myself. For I have prayed my GOOD ANGEL to speak for me, and he hath denied it. I have called upon REASON, DREAD, and CONSCIENÇE, and they have answered me full heavily that they be loth to accuse me, but excuse me they can not ; and alledgeth many a great, reasonable cause why, that I cannot say nay thereto. I have called upon my servants which were taken[2] me to rule and govern, and if they would answer for me [as I would answer for them,] and they answer me right shortly, and say : If they should say any good word for me they should not say truth of me, and casteth to me that peril, that nobody would give credence unto them if they would say well of me ; but call them flatterers, false dissimulers and favourers of sin.

Alas ! alas ! I have heavily dispended my long life that, in all this long time (I) have not purchased me one friend to speak for me. Had our Lord, of His most ample grace, ordained me immediately after my christendom to have died forthwith, I might say I had been born in a blessed hour. But would it please your goodness to speak for me, and understand[3] whether I shall have hardiness to make a bill to the

[1] *i.e.* unprovided with. [2] *i.e.* given.
[3] *i.e.* make me understand.

Blessed Lady, and most holy Virgin that ever was; and she that disdaineth not, nor denieth sinners when they call after grace, notwithstanding her chastity and her pure virginity excelleth all other virgins.

Now good,[1] go your way and let me wit how I shall speed. For all this time I live in such dread and fear that me were better to die anon than live any longer in [the dread that I am in. And also I have so great] dread and fear of the righteousness of Almighty God that I am almost dead for fear. For REASON, DREAD, and CONSCIENCE said to me shortly that the high Judge would not be partial, nor He would not be corrupted with goods, but He will minister to me justice certainly. But, and He intend to minister to me justice without favour, I would appeal to His mercies certainly; for other remedy is there none pardie. ORIGEN our Blessed Lady hath holpen, THEOPHIL and SIR EMORY;[2] how should they have done ne[3] the Mother of mercy had been? And many another sinner that her grace hath holpen. She is Queen of Heaven, Lady of the World, and Empress of Hell; and sithen her own Son, Our Lord Jesu Christ, hath died and suffered so tormentuous a death, and in her own sight, to her great sorrow and motherly compassion, I hope that she would be loth that thilk precious passion should be lost in any creature that her Blessed Son suffered so patiently.

[1] *i.e.* good Faith and Hope.
[2] de Worde, 'Thyophyle and Sir Emery.
[3] *i.e.* lest.

The Answer of Faith to the Dying Creature

Have ye none acquaintance with our brother Charity? We marvel that ye have not spoken of him in all this time; for, and he were joined with us twain, your message should be more acceptably heard many fold.

The lamentable Complaint of the Dying Creature to Faith, Hope, and Charity

Certainly I have but little dealed with him. I was never conversant with him. That me repenteth now, for I feel by you twain that he may do much in the High Court. I have more dealed with vengeance than I have with charity. For I would have been avenged upon every man by my will. When the people had slain my children, my kin, my friends, and robbed and spoiled myself; and certainly I would have been a-wroke[1] right fain, and I had had power to my will. But though my power were little, certainly I have hated them, and willed them to have been done to as they have done to me. And well I wot that is not the order of charity. But now heartily I cry God mercy, and our Blessed Lady, and you, holy Charity; and here, afore God, Our Blessed Lady, and you three, I forgive them all —and all mine enemies—that they have done against me, and will not be avenged though I might. And I pray you holy Charity, though it were long or I

[1] avenged.

were acquainted with you, be not the lother to do for me. I sore repent me that I have thus unreasonably and unwittingly absented me from you, and heartily I cry you mercy, and pray you of your charity to put out of your mind my presumptuous folly. For certainly I shall never do so more again, but in every thing that I have to do I shall desire your favour, succour, and counsel. And I utterly deny and defy VENGEANCE, and never to deal with him more, howsoever I be done to; but take it in patience and think, as me ought of right, that worse than I have been done to, I have deserved to be done to. But that is not the WORLD, for him have I served and pleased, and displeased Almighty God, that is Maker of all things, and His Holy Begotten Son, that conceived was of the Holy Ghost, and born of the pure and chaste Virgin, and died for our redemption. And I have grievously offended and broken His commandments in all things, knowing that I did not well; wherefore my peril is the more. Nor I have not called after the blessed Holy Ghost's grace, mercy, succour, and His help, when I have been in places of peril of deadly sin. Nor upon that most holy, pure, chaste, and excellent Virgin, and besought her of grace. And she turned her visage from me not from lack of faith, but that methought that her most excellent [charity and] chastity must of very right abhor my sins, and all things that I pleased the world with.

I know well that I have displeased Him that redeemed me with His precious passion; and this,

I wot well, deserved a greater punishment than I have yet suffered. And there, as me lacked suffisance and boldness to come in the presence of them that I have so grievously offended, will it please your goodness, FAITH, HOPE, and CHARITY, charitably to go before and be mean for me to the Mother of mercy and pity, that she will go for me to the glorious Trinity, and take you three with her. For well I wot the glorious Trinity will nothing deny that she desireth. They understand her perfect charity is such that every creature that calleth after grace, she hath pity upon them ; have they never so grievously offended. I should fall in despair and I had not perfect trust in her grace, mercy, and pity. And so I have great cause, for I have brought my seely[1] soul to great bondage, and in such adversity without remedy, that it passeth my power to ease him or help him, nor[2] the great nor special trust that I have in that most blessed Lady, and in you, holy FAITH, HOPE, and CHARITY.

HOW THE SORROWFUL SOUL COMPLAINETH HIM TO THE DYING CREATURE : SAYING RIGHT THUS

How much hast thou done with thy master, the WORLD ? How nigh be ye twain departed ? Understandest thou not how unsure he is, and at thy most need will fail thee ? Hast thou not seen, afore this time, in the times of great adversities and troubles,

[1] Here means 'poor,' "often used of the soul as in danger of divine judgment." O.E.D.

[2] except for.

what hath he eased or profited thee? Certainly little or nought. For, and he hath flattered or dissimuled with thee one day or one hour, he hath loured and grutched with thee[1] an whole year therefore. Hast thou not understood him in all this time, but hanged upon him always, so long as thou mightest; and longer wouldest if thou might? But now the season [and time] is come he will depart from thee; and what distress that ever thou art in, little will he savour, succour or help thee. Such as thou thinkest be thy friends will show thee a feigned favour, till they know the certainty of thy riches; and if thou have goods they will cherish and favour thee for a season, and complain and wail thy death. And yet they would right fain thou were a-gone, and be right glad of thy death. And when thine eyes be closed, thine hearing a-gone, thy speech withdrawn and may not speak, then shalt thou see what thy master the WORLD will do for thee. Seek thy coffers he will, and every corner by the way of likelihood where any goods is in. And little will thy worldly friends depart with[2] to thee then, and little compassion will they have on thy poor soul. And if they find little or nought in thy coffers, what will they say then? They will say thou were a fool, a waster; thou couldest not keep; thou spendest more than thou haddest. Thus will they say by thee. And though they find much, thou shalt have but a little thereof, and fare but little the better.

[1] *i.e.* frowned upon and complained of thee.
[2] *i.e.* divide.

And if they find but little, they will grudge with thee[1] and say thee never a good word.

Think thereon betimes, and be thine own friend; for, and thou canst not love thyself, who will love thee? Canst thou love every[2] creature better than thyself? If thou do so, I wis thou art not wise. Remember what I say now, for thou shalt find this true, every word. And though I speak thus grievously and straitly unto thee, marvel not for it; for he am I that shall abide and suffer, and endure the pains of thy distress. Alas that ever I was coupled with thee! And so have I cause to say, for I shall be punished without favour for thy deeds. How hastily, how soon [I cannot say. How unadvisedly and how unreadily thou purveyeth for me ;] I wot never. How should any other creature have compassion on me when thou hast not, that, sith that thou were first formed a creature, I have always been with thee and never from thee; and in the age of thine innocency was kept full virtuously to my great comfort; and in thy middle age was kept full viciously and sinfully to my great sorrow; and in thine old age little or nought remedied[3] thy wretched living.

Alas! Alas! Alas! that ever thou and I were coupled together! For the season hasteth fast that I must go to pains for thy misrule, and endure pain—whether it be eternal or for a long season. I wot not what remedy thy worldly friends will find to ease me. I am in great dread. I trow they will have little com-

[1] complain of thee. [2] de Worde, 'any.'
[3] de Worde, 'remembered.'

passion on me that am thy poor soul, but give their attendance to bury thee richly and worshipfully, and make thy house cleanly and thy purse empty; and little compassion or remembrance have on thee and me certainly, but let me burn eternally, but if[1] (by) the mercies of Him that is Almighty, (and) by the mean[2] of His most holy Mother; that pure, chaste, maiden that helpeth every sinner that calleth after grace when there is none other remedy.

Now farewell Body. Thou shalt to the Earth, and lie and rot, and worms eat thee; and I shall to pains long, or else eternal. Mercy, blessed Lady, that bare Christ Jesu, Our aller Redemptour: for in none other help I assure me.

The lamentable Lamentation of the Dying Body to the Soul

Alas, seely soul, the torments and pains of mine offences shall ye suffer. I am so sorry. There can no tongue tell the sorrow that I endure that have brought you in such bondage, peril, danger and adversity, without remedy; nor the high and mighty mercies of Almighty God, whose mercies cannot be had but by the mean of His Blessed Mother. And if she that is so chaste, so pure, and so holy, would abhor the abomination of our sins, what should we do? I have desired Faith, Hope, and Charity, to be mine advocates to her that bare Christ Jesu, and when I am answered again, such answer as I have I shall let you wit.

[1] *i.e.* except. [2] *i.e.* mediation.

How the Dying Creature complaineth Him to Faith, Hope, and Charity

O ye holy Faith, Hope, and Charity, where have ye been so long? I have lived in great dread how ye have sped. Have ye been with the Queen of Heaven, Lady of the world, and Empress of hell? That most glorious, pure, chaste virgin, that bare the Son of God that should redeem all mankind. How will her chaste and pure virginity receive me that am a sinner, and suffer me to come in her presence, and put a supplication to her most high, glorious, and excellent Prince, that have so grievously offended her blessed Son and her. Will she not abhor, nor disdain to look on me that am of all sinners the most horrible and abominable, and have so done that I cannot, without her most abundant grace, find a mean how to make aseth.[1] But I have heard say of old antiquity that she is so merciful and so gracious to sinners [when they call after grace, and hath holpen so many sinners] that of right must have perished n'ere her grace had been. But what comfort ye have of her most abundant grace I pray you let me wit, for certainly I live in great despair. For here hath been with me, sith ye went, my Soul, and complained that he must perish eternally in my default,[2] and crieth and waileth the time that ever he was coupled with thilk ungracious body, that so hath ruled him; and I can give him no comfort without you three.

[1] satisfaction. [2] *i.e.* for my failure.

The answer of Faith, Hope, and Charity to the Dying Creature

We, Faith, Hope, and Charity, have done your message, and found that Princess full graciously disposed; and saith that she remembereth well how the glorious Trinity chose her of one assent to be mediatrix and mean between God and man. And that her great worship and joy was caused for our redemption,—which she cannot put in oblivion; and also the great sorrows, not one but many, that she had at her blessed Son's passion, and saw her blessed and well-beloved Child die so tormentously for the redemption of sinners, and He guiltless Himself in everything, but of His great and most ample grace, mercy, and charity that He showeth to all sinners. And so precious, so glorious, and so tender was never none as He was. For He was the very pure Godhead, medled with her pure, chaste, virginity and maidenhood; and in her precious body made His holy habitation nine months; and in her soul eternally. And when she understood the prophecy, of her great meekness desired that she might be one of those and simplest servant, to her that should bare the Son of God and Him that should redeem all mankind: and her great meekness thought herself not worthy to that most holy occupation.

And therefore be of good chere, for we three, Faith, Hope, and Charity, will bring you there, and not leave you till ye be answered. And sith ye have put your special trust in us to be your advocates, and laid apart all temporal and worldly trust, we three will not fail you. And therefore put your soul in comfort, and arm you with the armour of a sure and holy CONFESSION, with a sorrowful CONTRITION, purposing to do very SATISFACTION; and be out of doubt. We hope ye shall speed right well, if it be in your heart as ye speak with your mouth,—and else trust not to our friendship in no wise. But go and labour your supplication as effectually as ye can devise, and be out of all despair; for we, FAITH, HOPE, and CHARITY, will believe [1] you for the trust that ye have had alway in us.

HOW THE DYING BODY CALLETH AFTER THE SOUL AGAIN

Where be ye, dear SOUL, that here was with me but late, complaining that ye must to pain for a long while or else eternally, and in my default and without remedy? I have been in such dread, sorrow, and fear for you that nothing could comfort me till FAITH and HOPE came to me and asked me if I were not acquainted with CHARITY. And I have answered them simply that I was never acquainted with him, and that me repenteth sore now. But Faith and Hope have brought me with him, and I have lowly and humbly submitted myself to him, and meekly cried him mercy of my presumptious folly; promising that I will never offend him more, denying all such as be his enemies, and as he loveth not

[1] de Worde, 'not leave you.'

vengeance, hatred, and cruelty, and promised him faithfully that I will never deal with them more; and I hope[1] he hath pardoned me. And (he) hath been in the company of FAITH and HOPE to the Mother of mercy for me, and brought me (a) right gracious answer again: That she cannot put in oblivion the great joy, worship, and comfort that she had of the Son of God for the redemption of us sinners, neither the maidenly and motherly compassion that she suffered for Him in the time of the most precious, painful, and bitter passion; and that I shall have[2] hardiness to come to the presence of that most royal and imperial Princess, and put a supplication to her.

And therefore be of good cheer and suffer your pains patiently, for though it be long I hope it shall not be eternally. And good, dear SOUL, while ye and I be together, or that we depart, purvey[3] in your wisdom some remedy—what can be to your ease—and I will be agreeable thereto. For were we twain once divided and departed, few or none would have compassion on your pain. See ye not how the WORLD loureth upon us now every day, and is ready to depart from us every day, for little thing or nought? And less would they do for us and we twain were departed. Therefore, dear SOUL, the remedies that may be found through your wisdom I pray you find them, and I shall be right fain to execute them. For I am at this hour as sorry as it is possible any

[1] *i.e.* trust. [2] *i.e.* must have.
[3] foresee or provide.

wretch to be, that have brought you in the peril and danger that ye be in, and as fain would be to do that (that) might ease you, and gladder than ever I was to do anything that hath hurt you.

How the Dying Creature putteth his Supplication to the Mother of Mercy, Mary, replete with Grace: Princess of Ruth, Mercy, and Pity, to whom all Sinners resorteth when they be succourless

Meekly beseecheth and sorrowfully complaineth your dreadful[1] suppliant, that all my life long unto my last age have lived and not obeyed the commandments of Almighty God in nothing; but misruled myself and my life in all the seven deadly sins, and sinfully and simply have occupied [my five wits, and set aside all virtues and used and occupied] all vices, and served the devil, the world and the flesh, having very knowledge both of good and evil: and knew well that what pleased them displeased God, but I dreaded to displease them. And now hath been a servant-of-arms with me, and laid upon me the mace of his office cruelly, and hath commanded me to make me ready every hour; for I shall not wit when I shall be called to my judgment.

The certainty of death hath brought me into so grievous an infirmity that none earthly medicine can cure me. Mine enemies be great in multitude, and have environed[2] me and all my defaults brought with

[1] *i.e.* full of dread. [2] de Worde, 'overcome.'

them, and I wot well they will accuse me. My worldly friends have forsaken me. I have cried and called after them to answer for me; and they have answered me full straitly and unfriendly that they neither dare nor can, nor will answer for me, nor excuse me; and shortly they be departed from me. My Good Angel first, Reason, Dread, and Conscience and my Five Wits, hasteth them from me-ward, and leaveth me destitute and alone: and where to have succour I wot not, nor help. But as it fortuneth me in good time, may I say, I met with Faith, Hope, and Charity; and they have promised me that they will speak to your most excellent benign grace and mercy for me: and so I trust they have. For certainly of your most pure, chaste virginity, and un-wemmed[1] maidenhead was I never in doubt, and I have hoped and trusted to your mercies always. I have heard say that ye be Mother of orphans, and I wis I am a very orphan, fatherless and motherless. Ye be comfort and succour to all those that be destitute, desolate, and succourless. I wis Lady, that am I. For I have neither help, succour, nor comfort of no creature, but only the trust that I have in your benign grace. Ye be guide to them that be out of the way and seek the means to come to the right way. Ah, blessed Lady, I have been so long out of the right way that I sore dread and fear to call upon you for grace: but as Faith, Hope, and Charity have put me in comfort how loth ye be to see your Son's precious passion lost in any creature, and they have given me hardiness to

[1] *i.e.* unstained.

call upon your most noble and benign grace. And so Lady, with humble, sorrowful, and dreadful heart and mind, I beseech your most benign grace, mercy, and pity, to set me in the right way of salvation and make me one of the partners of your Blessed Son's precious passion, and of your maidenly and motherly compassions. And as ye became borrow[1] for MARY EGYPTIAN to your Blessed Son, so good Lady be my borrow, that I shall never from henceforth wilfully offend your Blessed Son or you, but sore repent that ever I have heard or did anything that hath displeased your Blessed Son or you; being in will never to return to sin and wretchedness again, but rather to die than wilfully to do anything that would displease my Lord Christ Jesu, or you.

Now Princess, excelling in might and worthiness all creatures, as in dignity; mine heart's Lady, my worldly chief Goods, pray your Son to have mercy upon me, sith in all my greatest mischief[2] to your grace I fly. I can no further resort to find any consolation. And sith my hope and trust is only set in you, be my refuge now in this great tribulation, and cover my sinful SOUL with the mantle of your mercies, and set your Son's precious passion between me and eternal damnation. AMEN.

THE SUPPLICATION OF OUR LADY TO OUR LORD JESU HER SON FOR THE SICK CREATURE

O JESU, my LORD and GOD, and my most Blessed Son, in whom is all plenty of grace and of undoubted

[1] *i.e.* pledge. [2] *i.e.* need.

mercy to and for all sinners that with steadfast faith and assured hope devoutly call unto God for help and grace, and humbly beseech mercy and forgiveness of their misfaults and offences. To You[1] I come as a solicitor and beseecher for this sick creature, which right humbly and with sorrowful and contrite heart sueth continually for Your grace and pardon, that it may like You to incline You of Your wonted pity to his request and complaints, and graciously to consider his needs and causes.[2] He is sore abashed and discomforted[3] in himself, and as who saith utterly confounded; considering his grievous and deep sins by the which he hath provoked Your wrath and indignation, by the which he is also sore encumbered and standeth in great danger of his enemies;—and namely he feareth him of Your dreadful judgment. For well he witteth that if Ye do him justice he is but lost for ever.

Yet for all this he despaireth not of Your mercy, for he is in good opinion,[4] and trusteth to rejoice[5] Your pardon, and be reconciled to grace. Whereupon he sueth continually to You as he may and dare. For he knoweth himself deeply drenched in sin, and so sore elonged[6] from grace by sin that he thinketh himself unworthy to approach to offer his prayer. And therefore he sueth by means,[7] and

[1] The plural form *you* and *your* is often used in addressing God as sovereign.

[2] 'cause' here means sickness or disease.

[3] grieved.

[4] *i.e.* in good hope, or expectation.

[5] enjoy.

[6] removed.

[7] *i.e.* mediators.

especially by me to whom he calleth importunately, with piteous and elenge[1] voices; and ceaseth not, but continueth in sobbing and weeping so lamentably that my heart rueth to hear. And certes I can no longer me contain, but to instant[2] his prayers and to put in[3] Your grace for him. For he clepeth me the Mother of mercy, for encheson[4] that I bare You, which be the very Well and Fountain of mercy, and have it of unseverable property to be merciful to all sinners. And for this he challengeth me in manner, as though I should [owe] of duty to enterpart[5] my labours and prayers in this behalf with him and for him, and to sue for the hasty speed of his reconciliation; and that he letteth[6] not to put me in mind that I was ordained of God to be mean atwixt Him and man. And certes I allow well his mind therein, for true it is that I ought so to be; that likewise as Ye, my dear Lord and Son, descended from heaven to earth by me, and became partner of man's nature by me, so that all sinners that be not in state of grace should be reconciled and restored to grace by me, and be made partners of joy by me.

This is well signified in the figure of Aaron's rod which bare a flower miraculously, as Scripture witnesseth: the which rod signifieth me, like as the flower betokeneth You. For as a rod groweth directly upward and is the straight mean betwixt the root and the flower, and he that will climb to gather

[1] miserable; de Worde has 'waylinge voyces.'
[2] urge or press. [3] *i.e.* claim. [4] for reason.
[5] *i.e.* share. [6] here = ceaseth.

the flower must ascend by the rod, [or else bow the rod] and cause the flower to stoop; so he that willeth to arise from sin must rise by me, and he that will accline[1] Your grace and rejoice Your pardon, must bow me by prayer, that I may cause You to stoop; that is to say to incline to their prayers.

Lo thus, my dear Lord and Son, it is open and evident that I am ordained to reconcile man, and that it is in manner my duty and office for to do. Wherefore, sith this sick creature thus continually and undefatigably crieth to me with piteous and doleful complaint, and requireth me so straitly that I can no less do than put me in endeavour for him [and enterpart my labours with him for him]—and certes not only for his importunate suit and prayer, but also for other considerations reasonable and charitable that move me to tender and instant his causes.

The First Consideration

One is that he is allied right nigh to me by spiritual cognation;[2] for both we have one Father, that is God Which is our Father by creation and one Mother, the Church, which is our Mother by regeneration. Thus is he my brother, and I his sister. And now, my Lord, me seemeth right unfitting, me being a Queen, to see my brother a prisoner. I at liberty, and he in thraldom. I in bliss, and he in torment. Wherefore I am constained, as who saith by nature, to sue for his delivery and reconciling.

[1] *i.e.* bend towards. [2] *i.e.* kindred.

And this is one of the considerations that reasonably move me to sue for his pardon.

THE SECOND CONSIDERATION

Another is this: That sith it liked You, of Your great bounty and inestimable charity, for the reconciling of man, to take [of me Your handmaiden] flesh and blood to offer in sacrifice for the redemption of me and this creature,—and all other whom it hath and shall like You to call to Your faith; me seemeth I ought not, forasmuch as in me lieth, to see that thing miscarry which Ye have so preciously redeemed and bought, as dearly as Ye bought me and with the same flesh and blood which Ye took of me, Your humble creature and handmaiden.

THE THIRD CONSIDERATION

Another is this: I and every each (of) Your other creatures be for Your part bound to sue[1] the means to honour, worship, and glorify You,—in that we can or may. But so it is that in justifying this sinner, great honour and glory shall be to You and to Your saints: for Your Scripture saith: GAUDIUM EST ANGELIS DEI St Luke
SUPER UNO PECCATORE PŒNITENTIAM AGENTE. That is xv. 10.
to say: Joy and gladness is to Your angels the conversion of one sinner contrite and penitent. And in another place Your Scripture saith: MAGIS GAUDIUM St Luke
EST SUPER PECCATORE PŒNITENTIAM AGENTE, QUAM SUPER xv. 7.
NONAGINTA NOVEM JUSTIS. That is to say and to signify that more joy and honour is to God in

[1] *i.e.* pursue.

reconciling a sinner that is in full and assured purpose to persevere in grace, than in (a) great multitude of other righteous that never offended.

Wherefore my Lord as I am bound to glorify and honour You, so am I in manner bound to make instance[1] for reconciling of this Your creature; in the which thing Ye shall be greatly honoured and glorified. And these be the things that move me to instant and solicit his causes, and to endeavour[2] me for him.[3]

The Fourth Consideration

Furthermore I see in him great ability and likelihood to be that creature that may serve You, honour and glorify You. For he is entirely displeased with himself that he hath so grievously sinned and offended Your grace, and he is right heavy and contrite therefore; and he remembereth him many sithes of his old sins—not as delighting nor having pleasure in them, but to his shame and great remorse—and he hath them in perfect hatred, insomuch that he would not offend again in the least of them for all the world; and he hath fastened his intent and purpose to be hereafter all of other demeanour, through Your help and grace; and he will gladly do penance for that he trespassed; and he lowly submitteth him to the correction of Holy Church, and wilfully assenteth to pay the finance and suffer the penance attached by Your Church, and to do satisfaction as is for his

[1] urgent entreaty. [2] de Worde, 'submit.'
[3] Here the handwriting in the MS. changes.

frailties possible. And where, as he saith himself, (he is) not of ability nor power to do satisfaction as him ought, in that behalf he putteth himself wholly in Your grace, and remitteth him to Your great mercy and to the merits of Your passion ; which countervaileth and prevaileth all the penances and satisfaction that might [be] possible [for to] be done by all the world, from Adam to the last creature that shall be born. And he piteously crieth to me and beseecheth me to enterpose my merits atwixt Your judgment and him, and to offer in sacrifice for him the sobbings and sighings and sorrowful and lamentable tears that I wept for You in Your tender young age and childhood, when Simeon prophesied to me Your passion, and when I had lost You in Jerusalem ; and the sorrows that I suffered for You in time of Your painful and grievous passion, when the sword of sorrow pierced my heart. And certain I am right well content and glad so to do ; and I beseech You so to accept my merits for his, as his, as he goodly deserveth, and to set my sorrows and tears of pity in place of his penances and contrition.

Furthermore it might like you to consider the great labour and business of Faith, Hope, and Charity : and namely of Charity, which sueth for him continually and never is idle, but busy in labour for him. And she clepeth and calleth on me for him incessantly to see the expedition of his causes, and she undertaketh for his a-bearing.[1] And well Ye wot that her desire and prayer may not be void

[1] behaviour or endurance.

nor frustrate, but she must be graciously heard in all her goodly requests and desires. She hath also retained FAITH and HOPE on her part for this sick creature; and he hath professed to keep Your faith inviolably, and hath put him in full assurance of Your mercy. For though it so be that he see not in himself whereof he may trust to rejoice Your pardon, yet she showeth him that in You is so great promptness of mercy and continual custom, that Ye be [wont] and used alway to forgive, and have of natural property to be merciful to all sinful, that it maketh him bold to fasten the anchor of his hope in You; and (he) trusteth finally to make a voyage in the port of Your mercy.

THE CONCLUSION OF OUR LADY'S SUPPLICATION

Now my Lord, sith all the good abilities and dispositions to grace be in this creature by Your sufferance, there is no more to do but that Ye let descend Your grace to the vessel so disposed; and that Ye vouchsafe to suffer him rejoice Your pardon, and reconcile him to Your Church, and make him a member thereof, the sooner and speedier for this my prayer and bequest. I You beseech, my most dear Lord and Son, whom it hath liked You alway to hear graciously, and never suffer to depart [boteless] but liever[1] of my petition: for which be to You and Your most honourable and dread Father, with the Holy Ghost Your equal Peer, everlasting joy, honour, and glory. AMEN.

[1] *i.e.* gladder.

NOTE ON THE LAMENTATION OF THE DYING CREATURE

This is copied from the MS. Harl. 1706 (fol. 96). The author is unknown. The catalogue says "perhaps by Hampole," but I think little heed need be taken to the suggestion since most of the longer treatises in this manuscript are ascribed to Rolle of Hampole; such for example as *The Orologium Sapientiæ*, *The Craft of Dying*, *The Treatise of Ghostly Battle*, and *The Ladder of Four Rungs*; all of which have been proved not to be his.

The Lamentation of the Dying Creature is in a different and later hand than the first part of the manuscript, and its style leads us to think that it is of later date than the other treatises collected together in this volume. It is more nearly related to the Mystery Plays than any of the former. In the old printed edition of Wynkyn de Worde's which is in the Bodleian Library (Tanner 193) there is a rough wood-cut—repeated curiously on the reverse side of the same leaf—which is evidently a reproduction of the one chosen from the block-book *Ars Moriendi* as the frontispiece for this volume. In de Worde's illustration, however, the scrolls are left blank, and the demon wears a more revengeful expression on his face. There is also a tower in the background behind the crucifix (can this have any connection with the "toure of all toures"?) and a latticed window is seen in the corner of the picture. In other respects it follows the illustration from the block-book; Our Lady stands beside the bed, and the same figure, with a staff in his hand and sheep by his side, is depicted as in our frontispiece.

APPENDIX

(See note to p. 102)

SINCE writing the above note I have heard from the Librarian of the John Rylands Library that they possess a copy of this tract reprinted by Wynkyn de Worde in 1496, under the same title, viz.: "A lytell treatyse shortely compyled and called ars moriendi, that is to saye the craft for to deye for the helthe of mannes soule." Mr Guppy tells me it is "identically the same text as that contained in the unique copy in the Bodleian, which is without printer's name, date or place, but which is printed in Caxton type No. 6."

GLOSSARY

(When a word only occurs once in the text it will not be found in the glossary.)

advise, ponder, think on.
aggrieve, aggravate, make heavy.
allowing, praising, hallowing.
anon, immediately.
apparelled to, prepared to.
article, a critical point or moment; chiefly used of the moment of death.
assistant, standing by, present.

be-clip, embrace.
be-hest, a promise.
be-hight, promised.
be-hote, promised, vowed.
bote, remedy.
busy, careful, diligent.
but if, unless.

can, often means 'know.'
careful, sorrowful.
charging, accusing.
chere, countenance, face.
clepe, *clepen*, call.
clip, embrace, clasp.
comfort (*v.*), to strengthen.
commodity, convenience, supply of.

con (*v.*), to learn, be able to.
conversation, behaviour, life.
coude, knew.
covent, convent.
cunning, knowledge.

de-fault, failure.
de-fault of, lack of, absence of.
depart, divide, separate.
dilection, spiritual love.
dis-partle, scatter.
disposed, prepared.
dispose to (*v.*), prepare for.
doubt, dread.
dress (*v.*), prepare, direct.

enforce (*v.*), strive, exert.

faculty, resource.
fonde, foundation, source.
force, to give, to take heed to.
for-sloth, to lose through sloth.

glose (*v.*), flatter.
grin, a snare.

grint (*v.*), to gnash with the teeth.
grutch, i. complain, grumble; ii. grudge.
grutching, murmuring.

hasted, pressed, urged.
hasty, *hastily*, sudden, suddenly.

incontinent, straightway.
inconvenient, incongruous.
infounde, to shed into.
instance, entreaty.
instant (*v.*), to urge, entreat.

kind, nature.

let, *letted*, hinder, hindred.
letting, hindering, ceasing.
lewd, ignorant.
lewd man, layman.
lowable, deserving of praise.

may, generally equivalent to 'can.'
mean, mediator, mediation.
medled, mingled.
mischief, i. need, want; ii. misfortune, evil.
miserations, mercy, compassion.
mowe (*s.*), power, might.
mowe (*v.*), to be able.
movings, emotions, impulses.

namely, especially, particularly.

oftsithes, oft-times.
or, before.
otherwhile, at times.
out-take, except.

passing, surpassing.
pay, *payd*, to please, pleased.
perish, *perishing*, destroy, destroying.
plain, absolute.
plainly, fully, entirely.
point (*in a*), point of time, moment.
presently, without delay.
proper, own.
purvey, foresee, provide.
put, i. give, place; ii. ponder, consider.
put in, urge, claim.

rather, soon, earlier.
rejoice, enjoy.
reproachable, deserving of reproach.
require, request, desire.

sad, wise.
sadly, i. wisely; ii. constantly.
seely, i. holy, blessed; ii. poor, wretched.
sentence, meaning.
sith, *sithen*, since.
sithe, time.
slothed, delayed.
sort, lot.
spring, sprinkle.
suddenly, without delay, forthwith.
sue, pursue, follow.

take, often means 'receive,' 'give.'
thilk, the same.
thirl, *thrill*, pierce.

unbelapped, enwrapped.
uncunning, ignorance.
undisposed, unprepared.
unkindly, unnatural.
unneth, *unnethes*, seldom, scarcely.

very, real, true.

waymenting, lamenting.
wilfully, willingly.
wood, mad.
worship, honour.

CPSIA information can be obtained at www.ICGtesting.com
Printed in the USA
LVOW04s1408051114

412167LV00010B/86/P

9 781110 647149